Sigmund Freud
1856–1939

Sigmund Freud

The 'Wolfman'

[From the *History of an Infantile Neurosis*]

TRANSLATED BY LOUISE ADEY HUISH

PENGUIN BOOKS — GREAT IDEAS

PENGUIN BOOKS

Published by the Penguin Group
Penguin Books Ltd, 80 Strand, London WC2R ORL, England
Penguin Group (USA) Inc., 375 Hudson Street, New York, New York 10014, USA
Penguin Group (Canada), 90 Eglinton Avenue East, Suite 700, Toronto, Ontario,
Canada M4P 2Y3 (a division of Pearson Penguin Canada Inc.)
Penguin Ireland, 25 St Stephen's Green, Dublin 2, Ireland (a division of Penguin Books Ltd)
Penguin Group (Australia), 250 Camberwell Road, Camberwell, Victoria 3124, Australia
(a division of Pearson Australia Group Pty Ltd)
Penguin Books India Pvt Ltd, 11 Community Centre, Panchsheel Park,
New Delhi – 110 017, India
Penguin Group (NZ), 67 Apollo Drive, Rosedale, North Shore 0632, New Zealand
(a division of Pearson New Zealand Ltd)
Penguin Books (South Africa) (Pty) Ltd, 24 Sturdee Avenue, Rosebank, Johannesburg 2196,
South Africa

Penguin Books Ltd, Registered Offices: 80 Strand, London WC2R ORL, England

www.penguin.com

'Aus der Geschichte einer infantilen Neurose' first published 1918 in Freud,
Sammlung kleiner Schriften zur Neurosenlehre (Vienna, 1906–1922), 4
Sigmund Freud's German text collected in *Gesammelte Werke* (1940–52)
Copyright © Imago Publishing Co. Ltd., London, 1946
This translation first published in Penguin Classics 2002
This extract published in Penguin Books 2010

002

Tranlsation copyright © Louise Adey Huish, 2002

All rights reserved

The moral right of the translator has been asserted

Set in 11/13 Dante MT Std
Typeset by TexTech International
Printed in England by Clays Ltd, St Ives plc

ISBN: 978-0-141-19220-8

www.greenpenguin.co.uk

MIX
Paper from
responsible sources
FSC® C018179

Penguin Books is committed to a sustainable
future for our business, our readers and our planet.
This book is made from Forest Stewardship
Council™ certified paper.

Contents

Contents

I
Preliminary Remarks

The case of illness that I shall document in the following pages – once again only in fragmentary form – has a number of distinguishing peculiarities which demand some special comment before I embark on my account. The case concerns a young man who suffered a physical collapse in his eighteenth year following a gonorrhoeal infection; when, several years later, he came to me for psychoanalytic treatment he was completely dependent and incapable of autonomous existence. He had lived more or less normally during the decade of his youth which preceded the illness and had completed his secondary school studies without undue disruption. His earlier years, however, had been dominated by a serious neurotic disorder which began shortly before his fourth birthday as anxiety hysteria (animal phobia) and then turned into an obsessive-compulsive neurosis [*Zwangsneurose*], religious in content, the ramifications of which persisted into his tenth year.

I shall document only this infantile neurosis. Despite a direct demand to this effect on the part of my patient I have declined to write a complete history of his illness, treatment and recovery because I regard the exercise as technically impracticable and socially unacceptable. This deprives me of the possibility of demonstrating the connection between his childhood illness and the later, definitive episode. Of the latter I can say only that it caused our patient to spend long periods of time in German sanatoria where his case was classified by the highest authorities as 'manic-depressive psychosis'. This was an accurate diagnosis of the patient's father, whose life, rich in interests and activities, had regularly been disrupted by severe attacks of depression. As far as the son is concerned, however, I have been unable to observe, in the course of several years, any mood swings that go beyond what is consonant with the obvious psychic situation in terms of intensity and conditions of appearance. I have formed the impression that this case, like many others on which clinical psychiatry imposes a variety of changing diagnoses, is to be understood as a residual condition resulting from a case of obsessive-compulsive neurosis which has spontaneously run its course but where recovery has been incomplete.

My account will thus deal with an infantile neurosis analysed not during the course of the illness but fifteen years after it had come to an end. This situation has both advantages and disadvantages in comparison with the other. Analysis of the neurotic child himself will appear fundamentally more reliable but is unlikely to contain much by way of content; we have to put too many words and thoughts into the child's mouth and may perhaps find nevertheless that the deepest strata cannot be penetrated by consciousness. Analysis of a childhood illness via the medium of adult memory, where the individual is now intellectually mature, is free of such limitations; but we must take into account the distortion and adjustment that takes place when, at a later date, we look back at our own past. The former situation brings more convincing results, perhaps, but the latter is by far the more instructive.

In any case it is fair to say that the analysis of childhood neuroses can lay claim to a particularly high degree of theoretical interest. Such analyses do about the same for the proper understanding of adult neurosis as children's dreams do for the dreams of adults. Not that they can be seen through more easily or are composed of fewer elements; the difficulty of empathizing with the inner life [*Seelenleben*] of the child in fact makes such dreams particularly hard work for the physician. However, they dispense with so many of the subsequent layers that the essential elements of the neurosis emerge with unmistakable clarity. It is well known that resistance to the results of psychoanalysis has taken a new form in the present phase of the battle over psychoanalysis. Previously it was enough to challenge the reality of the facts asserted by analysis and to this end the best technique appeared to be to avoid any kind of verification. Apparently, this procedure is gradually being exhausted and opposition now takes a different route, acknowledging the facts but disposing of the resulting conclusions by means of re-interpretation so that it is possible, after all, to fend off such offensive conclusions. The study of childhood neurosis shows that these attempts at reinterpretation, which are either shallow or forced, are entirely inadequate. It demonstrates that the libidinal drives which my opponents would so like to deny are of paramount importance in the formation of neurosis, while revealing the absence of any pursuit of distant cultural goals, about which the child knows nothing and which can therefore have no meaning for him.

Another feature that commends the analysis described here to the reader's attention relates to the severity of the illness and the length of treatment required. Those analyses that lead quickly to a favourable outcome are valuable for the therapist's self-confidence and demonstrate the medical significance of psychoanalysis; but they remain of scant importance in promoting our scientific understanding. We learn nothing new from them. They lead so quickly to success only because we already knew everything that was necessary to deal with them. We can only learn something new from analyses that present us with particular difficulties, which can be surmounted only after some considerable time. In these cases alone do we succeed in descending to the deepest and most primitive strata of inner development in order to retrieve solutions to problems which are posed by the forms assumed subsequently by that very development. Strictly speaking we might then say that only an analysis that has penetrated thus far is worthy of the name. Of course, a single case cannot enlighten us with regard to everything we should like to know. Or, more precisely, it could tell us everything if we were only in a position to comprehend it all and if the unpractised nature of our own perceptions did not oblige us to be content with just a little.

The case of illness that I shall describe in the following pages left nothing to be desired in terms of productive difficulties of this kind. The first years of treatment produced very little change. A fortunate constellation decreed that external circumstances made it possible, nevertheless, to continue with the therapeutic attempt. I can easily imagine that in less favourable circumstances the treatment would have been abandoned after a certain period of time. I can only say in favour of the physician's standpoint that he must be as 'timeless' in his approach as the unconscious itself if he wants to learn or achieve anything. In the end this can happen only if he is prepared to renounce any short-sighted therapeutic ambitions. There are few other cases in which one can expect the degree of patience, submissiveness, insight and trust that were required on the part of this patient and those closest to him. The analyst can tell himself, however, that the results achieved in one case by such lengthy endeavours will now help significantly to reduce the treatment time in another, equally severe, case, and that in this way the timeless nature of the unconscious can progressively be overcome, once one has yielded to it on the first occasion.

The patient I am concerned with here maintained an unassailable position for a long time, entrenched behind an attitude of submissive indifference. He listened and understood but would allow nothing to come anywhere near him. One could not fault his intelligence, but it was as if it had been cut off by those involuntary [*triebhaft*] forces that determined his behaviour in the few human relationships left to him. He had to be educated for a long time before he could be persuaded to take an independent interest in our work and when, as a result of his efforts, the first moments of release occurred, he suspended the work immediately to prevent any further possibility of change and to maintain the comfortableness of the former situation. His timidity at the prospect

of an independent existence was so great that it out-
weighed all the hardships of being ill. There was only
one way of overcoming it. I had to wait until his attachment to me had grown strong enough to counterbalance
it, and then I played off the one factor against the other.
I decided – not without allowing myself to be guided by
reliable signs that the timing was right – that the treatment would have to end by a certain date, no matter
what progress had been made. I was determined to keep
to this deadline; in the end my patient recognized that I
was serious. Under the inexorable pressure of the deadline that I had set, his resistance, his fixed determination
[*Fixierung*] to remain ill gave way, after which the analysis
delivered up all the material which made it possible,
within a disproportionately short length of time, to dis-
solve his inhibitions and eliminate his symptoms. It is
from this last period of therapeutic work, during which
the patient's resistance had at times completely disap-
peared and he gave an impression of the kind of lucidity
normally only to be attained through hypnosis, that I
derived all the explanations which enabled me to understand his infantile neurosis.

In this way the course of the treatment illustrated the
dictum, long held to be true by the analytic technique,
that the length of the road that the analysis must travel
with the patient and the wealth of material that must be
mastered on that road are as nothing compared to the
resistance encountered during the work, and are only
worthy of consideration in that they are necessarily proportional to that resistance. It is the same process as when
a hostile army takes weeks and months to cross a stretch

of land that an express train could cover in a few hours in peace time, and that one's own army had crossed in a matter of days a short time before.

A third peculiarity of the analysis in question only compounded the difficulty of deciding whether to write about it. On the whole the results are satisfactorily congruent with what we already knew, or else a clear connection can be established. However, many details appear so curious and incredible, even to me, that I hesitate to ask others to give them credence. I exhorted my patient to subject his memories to the most rigorous criticism but he found nothing improbable in what he had said and maintained that he was telling the truth. My readers can at least be sure that I am merely reporting something that arose as an independent experience and was not influenced in any way by my expectations. I could not do otherwise than recall those wise words that tell us there are more things in heaven and earth than are dreamt of in our philosophy. Anyone capable of screening out his acquired convictions even more thoroughly than I could will no doubt discover still more of such matters.

II
Survey of the Patient's Milieu and Medical History

I can write neither a purely historical nor a purely pragmatic history of my patient; I can provide neither a treatment history nor a case history, but shall find myself obliged to combine the two approaches. It is well known that no way has yet been found to embed the convictions that are gained through analysis within any account of the analysis itself. Certainly nothing would be gained by providing exhaustive minutes of what took place during analytic sessions; moreover, the techniques of the treatment preclude the production of any such minutes. An analysis of this kind is not published, then, to command the conviction of those who have hitherto shown themselves to be dismissive and incredulous. We expect to offer something new only to those researchers whose experiences with patients have already sown the seeds of conviction.

I shall begin by describing the child's world and relating those aspects of his childhood story that I learned without any particular effort; essentially nothing was added to this material over several years, and it remained just as opaque during the whole of this time.

His parents married young; it was a happy marriage, but the first shadows were soon to be cast by illness on both sides, his mother suffering from gynaecological complaints, his father from attacks of moroseness which resulted in his absence from the family home. Only much later did our patient develop some understanding of his father's illness, of course, but his mother's ill-health was known to him from his earliest years. For this reason she had relatively little to do with her children. One day, certainly before the age of four, holding his mother's hand, he listens to his mother complaining to the doctor whom she is accompanying on his way, and commits her words to memory, later using them of himself. He is not the only child, but has a sister some two years older, lively, gifted and impetuously naughty, who is to play an important role in his life.

He is cared for by an old children's nurse as far back as he can remember, working-class, uneducated and untiringly affectionate towards him. For her he is a substitute for her own son, who died young. The family lives on a country estate which in the summer they exchange for another country estate. Neither is far from the city. It marks a turning-point in his childhood when his parents sell the estates and move to the city. Close relatives often come to stay on one or other estate for long periods of time, his father's brothers, his mother's sisters and their children, his maternal grandparents. In the summer, his parents used to go away for several weeks. In a cover-memory [*Deckerinnerung*] he sees himself standing with his nurse, watching his father, mother and sister being driven away in a carriage, and then going calmly back into the house. He must have been very small at the time. The next summer his sister was left at home and an

9

English governess appointed, whose responsibility it was to supervise the children.

In later years he was told a great many things about his childhood. Much of it he knew himself but without being able to make connections, of course, in terms of chronology or content. One story handed down in this way, which had been repeated in his presence on countless occasions because of his later illness, introduces the problem to whose solution we shall devote our attention. He is said to have been a very gentle, obedient and rather quiet child at first, so that people used to say he should have been the girl and his sister the boy. But once when his parents came back from their summer holiday they found him transformed. He had become discontented and irritable, was constantly flying into a passion, and would take offence at the slightest thing, raging and yelling like a savage, so that when this condition persisted, his parents expressed concern that it would not be possible to send him to school later on. It was the summer when the English governess was there; she had turned out to be a silly, cantankerous woman, and, incidentally, a slave to drink. His mother was thus inclined to see a connection between the boy's changed character and the English woman's influence, and assumed that he had been provoked by her treatment of him. His grandmother, a shrewd woman who had also spent the summer with the children, was of the opinion that the boy's touchiness was the result of constant quarrelling between the English governess and the children's nurse. The governess had repeatedly called the nurse a witch and obliged her to leave the room; the little boy had openly taken the part of his beloved 'Nanja' and made clear his hatred of the governess. Whatever the case, the English woman was sent away soon after the parents' return, without the child's disagreeable behaviour changing one whit.

The patient has retained his own memories of this difficult time. He thinks he made the first scenes when he did not receive two lots of presents at Christmas time, as he had a right to expect, Christmas Day being also his birthday. His beloved Nanja was not exempt from his demands or his touchiness, indeed she was perhaps the most relentlessly tormented of all. But this phase of character change is indissolubly linked in his memory to many other strange and morbid phenomena, which he is unable to bring into any kind of chronological order. He bundles together everything I shall be describing here, things that cannot possibly have occurred at the same time and that are full of internal contradictions, attributing them all to one and the same period of time, which he calls 'when we were still living on the first estate'. They left this estate, he thinks, when he was five years old. He is thus able to tell me that he suffered from an anxiety that his sister exploited in order to torment him. There was a particular picture book, which showed a picture of a wolf standing on its hind legs and stepping out. Whenever he set eyes on this picture he would start to scream furiously, fearing that the wolf would come and gobble him up. His sister, however, always managed to arrange matters so that he would have to see this picture and took great delight in his terror. At the same time he was also afraid of other animals, both large and small. On one occasion he was chasing after a lovely big butterfly with yellow-striped wings that had pointed tips, trying to catch it. (Probably a 'swallowtail'.) Suddenly he was seized by a dreadful fear of the creature and gave up his pursuit, screaming. He also experienced fear and disgust at the sight of beetles and caterpillars. And yet he was able to recall that at the same period he had tortured beetles and cut up caterpillars; horses also gave him an uncanny feeling. He would scream if a horse was beaten and once had to leave a circus for this reason. On other occasions he enjoyed beating horses himself. Whether these two conflicting attitudes to animals really held sway simultaneously, or whether one had not in fact supplanted the other – though if that were the case, in what order and when – his memory would not allow him to decide. He was also unable to say whether the difficult period was replaced by a period of illness or whether it had persisted throughout. In any case, in the light of what he went on to say, one was justified in making the assumption that in those childhood years he had gone through what could clearly be recognized as an episode of obsessive-compulsive neurosis. He told me that for a long period of time he had been very pious. He had had to pray at great length and cross himself endlessly before he could go to sleep at night. Every evening he would do the rounds of the holy pictures hanging in his room, using a chair to stand on, and bestow a reverent kiss on each one. It was somewhat out of keeping, then – or actually perhaps entirely in keeping – with this pious ritual that he recalled blasphemous thoughts coming into his mind, as if planted there by the devil. He was obliged to think: 'God – swine' or 'God – crud'. Once, journeying to a German spa, he was tortured by a compulsion to think of the Holy Trinity when he saw three piles of horse dung or other excrement lying on the road. At this time he used also to adhere to a peculiar ritual if he saw people who inspired pity in him, beggars, cripples, old men. He had to breathe out noisily in order not to become like one of them, and under certain conditions also had to inhale deeply. I was naturally inclined to assume that these clear symptoms of obsessive-compulsive neurosis belonged to a somewhat later period of time and a later stage of development than the signs of anxiety and the cruel behaviour towards animals.

Our patient's more mature years were characterized by a very unpromising relationship with his father, who after repeated depressive episodes could now no longer conceal the morbid aspects of his character. In the early years of his childhood it had been a most affectionate relationship, and this was how his son remembered him. His father was very fond of him and enjoyed playing with him. Even as a little boy he was proud of his father and would only ever say that he wanted to grow up to be a gentleman just like him. His Nanja had told him that his sister was his mother's child, but he was his father's, and this pleased him greatly. As his childhood came to an end he became estranged from his father. His father undoubtedly preferred his sister and he was very hurt by this. Later, fear of his father became the dominant emotion.

When he was getting on for eight all the symptoms the patient ascribed to the phase of existence which had begun with the difficult period disappeared. They did not disappear all at once but returned a few more times, finally ceding, in the patient's opinion, to the influence of the teachers and tutors who replaced his female carers. Put very briefly, then, the enigmas which yielded up their solutions in the course of the analysis are as follows: where did the boy's sudden change of character come from, what was the meaning of his phobia and his perversions, how did he acquire his compulsive [*Zwangs-*] piety and what was the connection between all these phenomena? Let me remind the reader once again that our therapeutic work was directed towards a later neurotic episode of recent occurrence and that information about those earlier problems could only emerge if the course of the analysis led us away from the present for a while, obliging us to take a detour through the pre-history of the patient's childhood.

III
Seduction and Its Immediate Consequences

Understandably my suspicions fell first on the English governess, whose presence in the house had coincided with the change in the boy. He had retained two cover-memories relating to her, which in themselves were incomprehensible. Once, as she was walking ahead of them, she said to the children following behind: 'Look at my little tail!' On another occasion her hat blew away when they were out on a trip, to the great satisfaction of brother and sister. These pointed towards the castration complex and might allow us to reconstruct, say, a threat made by her against the boy, contributing significantly to the development of abnormal behaviour. It is not in the least dangerous to put such reconstructions [*Konstruktionen*] to the analysand: they do no harm to the analysis if they are erroneous, and in any case one does not give voice to them if there is not some prospect of coming closer to the truth in the process. The immediate effect of putting forward these ideas was the appearance of dreams that it was not possible to interpret completely but which always seemed to play around with the same content. The subject of the dreams, as far as one could tell, was aggressive action on the boy's part towards his sister or the governess, which resulted in energetic rebuke and punishment. As if he had tried . . . after a bath . . . to expose his sister's nakedness . . . to tear off layers of clothing . . . or her veil . . . and the like. It was not possible, however, to arrive by means of interpretation at any definite content, and, once we had formed the impression that the same material was being processed in these dreams in ever-changing ways, it was clear how we were to understand what were apparently involuntary memories [*Reminiszenzen*]. It could only be a question of fantasies that the dreamer had once entertained about his childhood, probably during puberty, and which had now emerged again in a form so difficult to recognize.

We learnt what they meant in one fell swoop when the patient suddenly recalled the fact that his sister had seduced him 'when he was still very little, when they were living on the first estate' into sexual pursuits. First came the memory that on the lavatory, which the children often used together, she had issued the invitation: 'Shall we show each other our bottoms?' and had then suited the action to the word. Later we arrived at the more essential elements of the seduction and all the accompanying details of time and locality. It was in the spring, at a time when the father was away from home; the children were playing on the floor in one room while their mother was working in the next room. His sister had reached for his penis and played with it, saying incomprehensible things about Nanja all the while, as if by way of explanation. She said that Nanja did this all the time with everyone, the gardener, for example, she would turn him upside down and then take hold of his genitals.

This made it possible to understand the fantasies we

had guessed at earlier. They were intended to erase the memory of an event which later offended the patient's sense of masculine pride, achieving this goal by replacing historical truth with its wished-for opposite. According to these fantasies he had not taken the passive role towards his sister, but on the contrary had been aggressive, had wanted to see his sister without her clothes on, had been rejected and punished, and had thus fallen into the rage recounted so insistently by domestic tradition. It was also expedient to weave the governess into this story, since his mother and his grandmother attributed most of the blame to her, after all, for his bouts of rage. His fantasies thus corresponded exactly to the creation of sagas, by means of which a nation which later becomes great and proud seeks to conceal the insignificance and misadventure of its origins.

In reality the governess could have played only the most remote part in the seduction and its consequences. The scenes with his sister took place in the spring of that same year in which the English governess arrived to take the parents' place during the midsummer months. The boy's hostility to the governess in fact came about in a different way. By calumniating the children's nurse and saying she was a witch the governess was following in his sister's footsteps, since it was she who had first told him those dreadful things about their nurse, and this gave him the opportunity to express the repugnance that, as we shall learn, he had come to feel for his sister after she had seduced him.

That his sister had seduced him was certainly no fantasy, however. Its credibility was strengthened by a piece of information he received in later, more mature years and had never forgotten. In a conversation about his sister, a cousin, more than a decade older, had told him that he could remember very well what a forward, sensual little thing she had been. As a child of four or five she had once sat down on his lap and unfastened his trousers to take hold of his penis.

I shall interrupt the story of my patient's childhood for a moment in order to speak of this sister, her development, her subsequent fate and the influence she had over him. She was two years older and always ahead of him. Boisterous and tomboyish as a child, she underwent a dazzling intellectual development distinguished by an acute and realistic understanding; she favoured the natural sciences as an avenue of study yet at the same time produced poems of which their father had a very high opinion. She was intellectually far superior to her numerous early suitors and used to make fun of them. In her early twenties, however, she grew morose, complained that she was not pretty enough and withdrew from all social contact. Sent away on a tour in the company of an older lady, a friend of the family, she told the most improbable stories on her return of how her companion had ill-treated her, yet her inward attention remained obviously fixed on the woman who had allegedly tormented her. On a second journey, which took place soon afterwards, she poisoned herself and died a long way from home. Her state of mind probably corresponded to the onset of dementia praecox. Her case was among those testifying to a considerable inherited tendency to neuropathic affliction in the family, but it was by no means the only one. An uncle on the father's side, who lived for many years as an eccentric, died with every indication of having suffered from severe obsessive-compulsive neurosis; among the more distant relatives a considerable number have been and are afflicted by more minor nervous disorders.

In childhood our patient saw his sister – leaving aside for a moment the matter of the seduction – as an uncomfortable rival for their parents' approval and found the superiority that she so ruthlessly demonstrated highly oppressive. He particularly envied her the respect that their father demonstrated for her mental capabilities and her intellectual achievements, while he, inhibited intellectually since the episode of obsessive-compulsive neurosis, had to accept being held in lesser regard. From the age of thirteen onwards his relationship with his sister began to improve; similar intellectual aptitudes and shared opposition to their parents brought them so close that they were on the best and friendliest of terms. In the turbulent sexual agitation of puberty he ventured to approach her with a view to physical intimacy. When she rejected him with as much determination as skill he immediately turned from her to a young peasant girl, a servant in the house who bore the same name as his sister. In doing so he took a decisive step as far as his choice of heterosexual object was concerned, for all the girls he later fell in love with, often with the clearest signs of compulsion, were also servant girls, whose education and intelligence necessarily lagged far behind his own. We cannot deny that if all these objects of his love were substitutes for the sister who had refused him, then a tendency to demean his sister, to neutralize the intellectual superiority which had once so oppressed him, played a crucial part in his choice of object.

Alfred Adler subordinates everything, including the individual's sexual attitudes, to motives of this kind, arising from the will to power and the drive to assert oneself [*Behauptungstrieb*]. Without for a moment wishing to deny the validity of such motives of power and prerogative, I have never been convinced that they are able to support the dominant, exclusive role he attributes to them. If I had not seen the analysis of my patient through to the end, my observation of this case would have obliged me to modify my prejudice in the direction of Adler's theories. The concluding stages of the analysis provided unexpected new material, however, from which it became evident that these power motives (in this case, the tendency to demean) had only governed the patient's choice of object in the sense that they had contributed to it, rationalized it, while the real, more profoundly determining element allowed me to hold fast to my earlier convictions.

When news of his sister's death reached him, our patient told me that he felt barely a trace of pain. He forced himself into an outward show of mourning and was able coolly to rejoice in the fact that he was now the sole heir to the family fortunes. He had already been suffering from his more recent illness for some years when this occurred. I must admit, however, that this one statement made me hesitate in my diagnostic judgement of the case for some considerable time. True, it was to be supposed that his pain at the loss of the most beloved member of his family would be inhibited in its expression by continued jealousy towards her and the intrusion of his now unconsciously felt incestuous love, but I needed to find some kind of substitute for the outburst of pain that had failed to take place. I eventually found one in another expression of strong feeling, which had remained incomprehensible to him. A few months after his sister's death he had himself made a journey to the region where she had died; there he sought out the grave of a great poet whom at that time he idealized, and shed hot tears over the grave. He himself was perplexed by his reaction, for he knew that more than two generations had passed since the death of the poet he so admired. He understood what had happened only when he remembered that their father used to compare his dead sister's poems to those of the great poet. An error in his narrative had given me another indication as to the true meaning of this homage apparently paid to the poet, which I was able to draw his attention to at this point. He had repeatedly told me earlier that his sister had shot herself and then been obliged to correct himself, since she had taken poison. The poet, however, had been shot, in a duel.

I shall now take up the brother's story again, and for a while I must describe what actually took place. It turned out that at the time when his sister set about seducing him the boy was 3¼ years old. It happened, as I have said, in the spring of that same year in which his parents found him so radically changed on their return home in the autumn. It seems obvious, then, to assume that there was some connection between this transformation and the awakening of sexual activity that had taken place in the intervening period.

How did the boy react to his older sister's enticements? The answer is that he rejected her, but he rejected the person, not the thing. His sister was not acceptable to him as a sexual object, probably because rivalry for their parents' love had already determined his relationship with her as a hostile one. He avoided her and her advances soon ceased. In her place, however, he sought to win for himself another, more beloved person, and the things his sister herself had said, invoking Nanja as her model, guided his choice towards Nanja. He thus began to play with his penis in front of Nanja, something that must be taken, as in so many other cases where children do not conceal masturbation, as an attempt at seduction. Nanja disappointed him, telling him with a serious expression that that was a naughty thing to do. Children who did that would get a 'wound' there.

We can trace the effect of this remark, which was to all intents and purposes a threat, in various directions. His attachment to Nanja became less strong. He could have been angry with her; later, when the tantrums began, it became clear that she had indeed enraged him. Yet it was characteristic of him that initially he would stubbornly defend against anything new, whatever libido position he was having to give up. When the governess took the stage and insulted Nanja, driving her out of the room and trying to destroy her authority, he in fact exaggerated his love for the person under threat and behaved negatively and defiantly towards the attacking governess. Nevertheless he began secretly to look for another sexual object. The seduction had given him the passive sexual objective of having his genitals touched; we shall learn in due course the person with whom he hoped to achieve this and the paths that led to his choice.

It is entirely in accordance with our expectations to learn that his sexual inquiries began with his first experiences of genital arousal and that he soon came up against the problem of castration. At this time he had the opportunity to watch two girls urinate, his sister and her friend. He was bright enough to have been able to grasp the true state of affairs from this alone but instead behaved in the same way as we know other male children to behave. He rejected the idea that he was seeing confirmation here of the wound with which Nanja had threatened him, and explained it to himself as the girls' 'front bottom'. This decision did not mark the end of the subject of castration, however; he found new indications of it in everything he heard. Once, when sticks of barley sugar were handed out to the children, the governess, who was inclined to lurid fantasies, declared that they were chopped-up pieces of snake. This caused him to remember that his father had once come upon a snake when out for a walk and had chopped it into pieces with his walking-stick. He had been told the story (from *Reineke Fuchs* [*Reynard the Fox*]) where the wolf tried to catch fish in winter and used his tail as bait, whereupon his tail froze in the ice and broke off. He learnt the different names used for horses depending on the intactness of their sex. He was thus preoccupied with the thought of castration without believing in it or being frightened by it. Other problems relating to sexuality were posed by the fairytales with which he became acquainted at this time. In 'Little Red Riding Hood' and 'The Seven Little Kids' children were pulled out of the body of the wolf. Was the wolf female, then, or could men also carry children in their bodies? At this time he had not yet decided on the answer to that question. He had no fear of wolves as yet, incidentally, at the time of these investigations.

One remark made by our patient will clear the way to an understanding of the change in character that manifested itself during his parents' absence and that was distantly connected with his sister's seduction. He relates that soon after Nanja had rejected and threatened him he gave up masturbation. *The sexual life directed by the genital zone, which was beginning to stir, had succumbed to external inhibition, and this influence had flung it back into an earlier phase of pre-genital organization.* As a result of the suppression of masturbation, the boy's sexual life became anal-sadistic in character. He became irritable and took pleasure in tormenting animals and people, using this to achieve satisfaction. The principal object of torment was his beloved Nanja, whom he knew how to torture until she burst into tears. In this way he took his revenge for the rejection he had received at her hands, and at the same time satisfied his sexual desires in a form corresponding to this regressive phase. He started to be cruel to tiny creatures, catching flies so that he could pull off their wings, stamping on beetles; in his imagination he also enjoyed beating large animals, horses. These were entirely active, sadistic pursuits; we shall hear something of his anal impulses during this period in another context.

It is valuable to learn that fantasies of a quite different

kind, contemporaneous with these, also surfaced in the patient's memory, the content of which was that boys were being punished and beaten, beaten in particular on the penis; and we can easily guess for whom these anonymous objects served as whipping-boys by looking at other fantasies, which took the form of the heir-apparent being locked in a narrow room and beaten. He himself was obviously the heir-apparent; in his imagination his sadism was turned against himself, veering into masochism. The detail of the sexual organ itself taking its punishment allows us to conclude that a sense of guilt, directed at his masturbation, was already at work in this transformation.

In analysis there could be no doubt that these passive aspirations [*Strebungen*] emerged at the same time as, or very soon after, the active, sadistic ones. This is in keeping with an uncommonly distinct, intense and persistent *ambivalence* on the part of the patient, expressing itself here for the first time in the symmetrical development of contradictory pairs of partial drives. This behaviour was in future to remain as characteristic of him as the further trait that none of the libido positions which he achieved was ever in fact fully superseded by a later one. Each would exist alongside all the others, allowing him to vacillate unceasingly in a way that proved incompatible with the acquisition of a fixed character.

The boy's masochistic tendencies bring us to another point, which I have not mentioned up until now because it can only be firmly established through analysis of the subsequent phase of development. I have already mentioned the fact that, after Nanja rejected him, he broke away from her and focused his libidinal expectations on a different sexual object. This person was his father, then absent from home. He was guided towards this choice, no doubt, by the coincidence of various factors, including chance ones such as his memory of the dismembered snake; above all, however, he was renewing his first, original choice of object, which had been made, in accordance with the narcissism of the small child, by way of identification. We have already heard that his father had been a much-admired example to him, and that when asked what he wanted to be he used to answer: 'A gentleman like my father.' The object of identification in his active current [*Strömung*] now became the sexual object of a passive current in the anal-sadistic phase. We gain the impression that his sister's seduction of him had forced him into a passive role and given him a passive sexual objective. Under the continuing influence of this experience, he followed a path from sister to Nanja to father, from the passive attitude towards a woman to the same towards a man, and yet in doing so he was able to connect up with an earlier, spontaneous stage of development. The father was once again his object, identification having been succeeded by object-choice, as is appropriate at a higher stage of development; transformation of an active attitude into a passive one was both outcome and sign of the seduction that had taken place in the intervening period. Taking an active attitude towards the excessively powerful figure of the father during the sadistic phase would of course have been much less feasible. On his father's return, in late summer or autumn, his tantrums and furious scenes were put to a different use. They had served an active, sadistic purpose towards Nanja; now, towards his father, their purpose was masochistic. By parading his difficult behaviour he wanted to compel his father to punish and beat him and in this way gain from him the masochistic sexual satisfaction he desired. His screaming fits were nothing other than attempts at seduction. In accordance with the motivation behind masochism, he would also have found satisfaction for his sense of guilt in being punished. One memory had stored up a recollection for him of how, during one such exhibition of difficult behaviour, his screaming gets louder as soon as his father comes in; yet his father does not beat him but attempts to calm him down by throwing the cushions from the bed up in the air and catching them again.

I do not know how many times, in the face of a child's inexplicable naughtiness, parents and mentors would have occasion to recall this typical connection. The child who is behaving so wildly makes a confession, intending to provoke punishment. In being punished the child is seeking both the appeasement of its sense of guilt and the satisfaction of its masochistic sexual aspirations.

We owe the further clarification of this case to a memory, which came to the patient with great certainty, that the symptoms of anxiety had only joined the other signs of character change once a certain incident had occurred. Before then there had been no anxiety; immediately after this occurrence he found himself tormented by anxiety. We can state with certainty that the point at which this transformation took place was just before his fourth birthday. Thanks to this clue, the period of childhood with which we are particularly concerned can be divided into two phases, a first phase of difficult behaviour and

perversity which lasted from his seduction at the age of
3¼ until his fourth birthday, and a longer, subsequent
phase dominated by the signs of neurosis. The incident
that permits us to draw the dividing line was no external
trauma, however, but a dream, from which he awoke
beset with anxiety.

IV
The Dream and the Primal Scene

I have already published this dream elsewhere because of the fairytale elements it contains and so I shall begin by reproducing what I wrote at that time:

'I dreamed that it is night and I am lying in my bed (the foot of my bed was under the window, and outside the window there was a row of old walnut trees. I know that it was winter in my dream, and night-time). Suddenly the window opens of its own accord and, terrified, I see that there are a number of white wolves sitting in the big walnut tree outside the window. There were six or seven of them. The wolves were white all over and looked more like foxes or sheepdogs because they had big tails like foxes and their ears were pricked up like dogs watching something. Obviously fearful that the wolves were going to gobble me up I screamed and woke up. My nurse hurried to my bedside to see what had happened. It was some time before I could be convinced that it had only been a dream, because the image of the window opening and the wolves sitting in the tree was so clear and lifelike. Eventually I calmed down, feeling as if I had been liberated from danger, and went back to sleep.

'The only action in the dream was the opening of the window, for the wolves were sitting quite still in the branches of the tree, to the right and left of the tree trunk, not moving at all, and looking right at me. It looked as if they had turned their full attention on me. – I think that was my first anxiety-dream. I was three or four at the time, certainly no more than five. From then on until I was ten or eleven I was always afraid of seeing something terrible in my dreams.'

He then drew a picture of the tree with the wolves sitting in it, too, which confirms the description he gave [Fig. 1]. Analysis of the dream brought the following material to light.

He always related this dream to the memory that in those childhood years he would express a quite monstrous anxiety at the picture of a wolf that was to be found in his

Fig. 1

book of fairytales. His elder sister, highly superior, would tease him by showing him this very picture on some pretext or other, at which he would begin to scream in horror. In this picture the wolf was standing on his back paws, about to take a step forward, paws outstretched and ears pricked. He thought this picture was there as an illustration to the fairytale 'Little Red Riding Hood'.

Why are the wolves white? That makes him think of the sheep which were kept in large flocks quite near the estate. His father sometimes took him to visit the flocks of sheep and he was always very proud and happy when this happened. Later on – inquiries suggest that it could easily have been shortly before this dream took place – an epidemic broke out among the sheep. His father sent for one of Pasteur's disciples, who inoculated the sheep, but after the inoculation they died in even greater numbers than before.

How did the wolves get up in the tree? A story occurs to him that he had heard his grandfather tell. He cannot remember whether it was before or after the dream, but the content of the story strongly supports the first possibility. The story goes as follows: a tailor is sitting in his room working when the window opens and in leaps a wolf. The tailor hits out at him with his measuring stick – no, he corrects himself, he grabs him by the tail and pulls it off, so that the wolf runs away, terrified. Some time later the tailor goes into the woods and suddenly sees a pack of wolves coming towards him, and so he escapes from them by climbing up a tree. At first the wolves do not know what to do, but the maimed one, who is also there and wants his revenge on the tailor, suggests that one should climb on another's back until the last one can reach the tailor. He himself – a powerful old wolf – will form the base of this pyramid. The wolves do as he says, but the tailor recognizes the wolf who visited him, the one he punished, and he calls out suddenly, as he did before: 'Grab the grey fellow by the tail.' The wolf who has lost his tail remembers what happened, and runs away, terrified, while the others all tumble down in a heap.

In this story we find the tree that the wolves are sitting on in the dream. There is also an unambiguous link with the castration complex, however. It is the *old* wolf who loses his tail to the tailor. The foxtails which the wolves have in the dream are no doubt compensation for the absence of a tail.

Why are there six or seven wolves? It seemed that we could not answer this question, until I expressed some doubt as to whether his anxiety-image could in fact have referred to the tale of 'Little Red Riding Hood'. That fairytale gives rise to only two illustrations, the meeting of Little Red Riding Hood and the wolf in the forest, and the scene where the wolf is lying in bed wearing Grandmother's nightcap. Another fairytale must therefore be concealed behind his memory of that picture. He soon found that it could only be the story of 'The Wolf and the Seven Little Kids'. Here we find the number seven, and also the number six, for the wolf gobbles up only six of the little kids while the seventh hides in the clock-case. We also find white in this story, for the wolf has the baker whiten his paws after the little kids recognize him on his first visit by his grey paw. The two fairytales have a great deal in common, incidentally. In both we find people being eaten up, the stomach being cut open, the people who have been eaten taken out again, heavy stones being put back in their place and finally the big bad wolf being killed in both cases. In the story of the little kids we find the tree as well. After he has eaten his fill the wolf lies down under a tree and snores.

I shall have a particular reason to concern myself with this dream in another context, where I shall evaluate it and consider its possible meaning in greater depth. It is a first anxiety-dream, remembered from childhood, the content of which gives rise to a very particular sort of interest in the context of other dreams which followed soon after, and certain incidents in the dreamer's childhood. Here we shall confine ourselves to the dream's relationship to two fairytales which have a great deal in common, 'Little Red Riding Hood' and 'The Wolf and the Seven Little Kids'. The impression left on the child dreamer by these fairytales found expression in a veritable phobia about animals, distinguished from other similar cases only by the fact that the animal that gave rise to the anxiety was not a readily accessible object (such as a horse or a dog) but one familiar only from stories and picture books.

I shall look at the explanation for these animal phobias and the significance that we should attribute to them on another occasion. Here, I shall anticipate myself only by remarking that this explanation is entirely in keeping with the main characteristic which the dreamer's neurosis reveals in later life. Fear of the father was the most powerful motive for his illness and an ambivalent attitude towards any father-substitute dominated his life, just as it dominated his behaviour in the consulting room.

If, in my patient's case, the wolf was merely the first father-substitute, the question arises as to whether the secret content of the tale of the wolf who gobbled up the little kids or the tale of Red Riding Hood is anything other than infantile fear of the father. My patient's father, incidentally, had a characteristic tendency to '*affectionate scolding*', of the kind used by many people in dealing with their children, and the teasing threat 'I'll gobble you up' may have been uttered more than once when the father, later so strict, used to cuddle and play with his little son. One of my patients told me that her two children were never able to feel really fond of their grandfather because he used to frighten them, in the course of his affectionate games, by telling them he would cut open their tummies.

Leaving aside everything in this essay that anticipates how we might apply the dream, let us return to the immediate issue of how we should interpret it. I should point out that to arrive at an interpretation was an exercise that took several years. The patient told me about the dream very early on, and quickly embraced my conviction that it concealed the cause of his infantile neurosis. In the course of the treatment we often came back to the dream but only arrived at a complete understanding of it during the last months of the therapy, thanks to spontaneous work on the part of my patient. He had always emphasized that two moments in the dream had made the most powerful impression on him, first, the utter calm of the wolves, their motionless stance, and, second, the tense attentiveness with which they all stared at him. The sense of reality as the dream came to an end, which persisted after he had woken up, also seemed noteworthy to him.

Let us take up this last point. Experience of the interpretation of dreams tells us that there is a particular meaning to this sense of reality. It assures us that something in the latent material of the dream lays claim to reality in the dreamer's memory, and thus that the dream refers to an incident that actually took place and has not merely been fantasized. I am referring, of course, only to the reality of something unknown; the conviction, for example, that his grandfather really told him the story of the tailor and the wolf, or that the tale of 'Little Red Riding Hood' or 'The Seven Little Kids' had really been read to him could never be replaced by that sense of reality which outlasts the dream. The dream appeared to point to an incident the reality of which is emphasized by its very contrast with the unreality of the fairytales.

If we were to assume the existence of an unknown scene of this kind, concealed behind the content of the dream, i.e. a scene which had already been forgotten at the time of the dream, it must have occurred at a very early age. The dreamer tells us after all that 'when I had the dream I was three or four, certainly no more than five'. We might add, 'And the dream reminded me of something that must have taken place even earlier.'

Those aspects of the manifest dream-content singled out by the dreamer, the moments of attentive watching and motionlessness, had to lead us to the content of that scene. We naturally expect this material to be distorted in some way, perhaps even to be distorted into its opposite, as it reproduces the unknown material of the scene.

It was possible to draw a number of conclusions from the raw material provided by the first analysis, conclusions that could be fitted into the context we were seeking. Concealed behind the mention of sheep-breeding we could find evidence for his exploration of sexuality, interests that could be satisfied in the course of the visits he made together with his father; but there must also have been hints of a fear of death, since for the most part the sheep died in the epidemic. What stands out most in the dream, that is, the wolves in the tree, led directly to the grandfather's story, the most gripping aspect of which could hardly have been anything other than its connection with the topic of castration, the stimulus for the dream.

The first, incomplete analysis of the dream had further led us to infer that the wolf was a father-substitute, so that this first anxiety-dream had brought to light the fear of his father, which was to dominate his life from then on. It is true that even this conclusion was not yet a definite one. However, if we assemble the elements that can be deduced from the material provided by the dreamer, the results of the preliminary analysis, we find the following fragments, which could be used as the basis of a reconstruction:

An actual event – occurring at a very early age – watching – motionlessness – sexual problems – castration – the father – something terrible.

*

36

One day our patient took up the interpretation of the dream once again. He thought that the part of the dream in which 'suddenly the window opens of its own accord' is not entirely explained by its relation to the window at which the tailor is sitting and through which the wolf comes into the room. He thought it must mean: my eyes are suddenly opened. I am asleep then, and suddenly wake up, and then I see something: the tree with the wolves. There was nothing to object to here, but we could take it further. He had woken up, and had seen something. The attentive gaze, which in the dream he attributes to the wolves, is actually to be ascribed to him. At a decisive point a reversal [*Verkehrung*] had taken place, indicated, incidentally, by another reversal in the manifest content of the dream. For it is a reversal for the wolves to be sitting in the tree, whereas in the grandfather's story they are down below and are unable to climb up into the tree.

Now, what if the other moment emphasized by the dreamer had also been distorted by reversal or inversion [*Umkehrung*]? Instead of absence of motion (the wolves sit there motionless, gazing at him but not moving) we should have: violent movement. He woke up suddenly, then, and saw a scene of violent excitement which he watched with tense attentiveness. In the one case distortion consists in the exchange of subject and object, active and passive modes, being watched instead of watching; in the other case it consists in transformation into the opposite: calm instead of excitement.

Further progress in understanding the dream was made on another occasion by the abruptly surfacing notion that the tree was the Christmas tree. And now he knew that he had dreamed the dream shortly before Christmas, in anticipation of Christmas itself. Since Christmas Day was also his birthday it was now possible to establish a definite time for the dream and the transformation which it brought in its wake. It was shortly before his fourth birthday. He had fallen asleep in excited anticipation of the day that was to bring him two lots of presents. We know that, in circumstances like these, the child readily anticipates the satisfaction of his wishes in dreams. And so in the dream it was already Christmas, and the content of the dream showed him his presents, the gifts that were intended for him hanging on the tree. But instead of presents they had turned into – wolves, and the dream ended with his fear that the wolf (probably his father) would gobble him up, so that he sought refuge with his nurse. Our knowledge of his sexual development before the dream took place makes it possible for us to fill in the gap in the dream and explain the way in which satisfaction was transformed into fear. Among the wishes that informed his dreams, the strongest one that stirred must have been for the sexual satisfaction he longed to receive from his father. The strength of that wish succeeded in refreshing the long-forgotten memory trace [*Erinnerungsspur*] of a scene that could show him what sexual satisfaction from his father looked like, and the result was fright, horror at the satisfaction of his wish, repression of the impulse represented by the wish and therefore flight from the father towards the less dangerous figure of the nurse.

The significance of this Christmas date had been preserved in the alleged memory that his first tantrum had occurred because he had not been satisfied by his Christmas presents. This memory draws together true and false elements: it could not hold true without some modification since his parents had frequently repeated their assurance that his difficult behaviour had already been apparent after their return in the autumn and not just at Christmas; but the crucial aspect, the relationship between tantrums, Christmas and a lack of sexual satisfaction, had been established in this memory.

What was the image, however, conjured up by those sexual yearnings at work in the night, an image capable of scaring him away so powerfully from the fulfilment he desired? According to the material provided by the analysis there was one condition it had to fulfil: it had to be of a kind which would convince him of the existence of castration. Castration anxiety then became the driving force behind the transformation of his feelings.

We are now approaching the point at which I must abandon my attempt to draw on the actual course of the analysis. I fear that it will also be the point at which the reader will abandon his faith in what I have to say.

What was activated that night out of the chaos of unconscious traces left by a memory imprint [*Eindruck*] was the image of coitus between the boy's parents in conditions which were not entirely usual and which lent themselves to observation. It gradually became possible to find satisfactory answers to all the questions that might be prompted by this scene, given that that first dream was reproduced endlessly in countless variations during the therapy, and on each occasion the analysis provided the wished-for explanations. In this way we were first able to establish the child's age when he observed his parents, some 18 months. At the time he was suffering from malaria, and the attacks recurred at a certain time each day. From the age of nine onwards he was periodically subject to depressive moods, which would set in during the afternoon, reaching their lowest point at around five o'clock. This symptom was still present during the analytic treatment. The recurrent depression replaced the previous attacks of fever or lassitude; five o'clock was either the time when the fever reached its height or the time when he observed the coitus, supposing that the two did not coincide. He was probably in his parents' bedroom precisely because he was ill. This episode of illness, which is also directly corroborated by tradition, suggests that the incident took place in the summer, so that we can assume an age of n + 1½ for the boy born on Christmas Day. He had thus been asleep in his cot in his parents' room and woke up, possibly as a result of mounting fever, in the afternoon, perhaps at five o'clock, the hour that was later to be marked by depression. It would be in accordance with our assumption that it was a hot summer's day if his parents had retired for an afternoon siesta, only half dressed. On waking, he witnessed 'coitus a tergo' [from behind], repeated three times; he could see his mother's genitals as well as his father's penis and understood what was happening as well as what it meant. Eventually he disturbed his parents' intercourse in a way that will be discussed later.

Fundamentally, there is nothing out of the ordinary, nothing that gives the impression that we are dealing here with the product of wild imaginings, in the fact of a young married couple, married only a few years, allowing a siesta on a hot summer's day to evolve into tender relations, ignoring as they did so the presence of the 18-month-old boy asleep in his cot. I would say rather that it is entirely banal, an everyday occurrence, and even the coital position that we must infer does not alter this judgement in any way. Particularly since there is nothing in the evidence to suggest that coitus took place each time from behind. A single occasion would have sufficed, after all, to allow the spectator the opportunity to make observations that would have been rendered more difficult, impossible even, if the lovers had assumed a different position. The content of the scene itself is thus no argument against its credibility. The suspicion of improbability will be raised on three other counts: that at the tender age of 18 months a child should be capable of perceiving such a complicated event and retaining it so accurately in the unconscious; second, that it is possible at the age of 4 to process the memory imprints received in this way, belatedly advancing to an understanding of what was seen; and, finally, that the child should succeed by whatever method in making conscious the details of such a scene, witnessed and understood in such circumstances, in a way that is both coherent and convincing.

Later I shall subject these and other misgivings to careful scrutiny; let me assure the reader that I am no less critical than he in my acceptance of the child's observation, and would ask him to join me in resolving to believe *provisionally* in the reality of this scene. Let us first continue to study the way in which this *'primal scene'* [*Urszene*] is related to the patient's dream, his symptoms and his life history. We shall then consider separately the effects proceeding from the essential content of the scene and from one of the visual imprints contained in it.

By this last I mean the positions he saw his parents assume, the man upright and the woman bent over, rather like an animal. We have already heard how his sister used to scare him during his period of great anxiety by showing him the picture in his fairytale book in which the wolf is depicted standing on his hind legs with one foot forward, paws outstretched and ears pricked. While in therapy with me he never tired of searching in antiquarian bookshops until he found his childhood picture-book and recognized in one of the illustrations to 'The Tale of the Seven Little Kids' the image that had so terrified him. He thought that the position assumed by the wolf in this picture might have reminded him of the position taken by his father in the primal scene we had reconstructed. At any rate, this picture was the starting-point for a further backwash of fear. On one occasion, at the age of six or seven, when he learned that he was to have a new teacher the next day, he dreamed the following night that this teacher was a lion and was approaching his bed, roaring loudly, in the stance taken by the wolf in the picture, and once again awoke in terror. By then he had already overcome the wolf phobia and so was free to choose another animal as the object of his anxiety; in this later dream he recognized that the teacher was a father-substitute. Each of his teachers played this same paternal role in the later years of his childhood and was vested with the influence wielded by his father for good and ill.

Fate gave him strange cause to renew his wolf phobia

during his grammar school years, and to make the relationship underlying it a channel for serious inhibitions. The name of the teacher responsible for Latin instruction in his class was *Wolf*. He was intimidated by this man right from the start and was once resoundingly told off by him for making a stupid mistake in a Latin translation, after which he could not shake off the paralysing anxiety this teacher induced in him, soon transferred on to other teachers as well. The occasion on which he came to grief in his translation is not without significance, however. He had to translate the Latin word 'filius' and did so using the French word 'fils' instead of the corresponding word in his own tongue. The wolf was indeed still the father.

The first of the 'transitory symptoms' that the patient produced during treatment in fact went back to the wolf phobia and the tale of 'The Seven Little Kids'. In the room where the first sessions took place there was a large grandfather clock opposite the patient, who lay on a divan with his head turned away from me. I was struck by the fact that, from time to time, he would turn his face towards me, look at me in a very friendly way, as if to placate me, and then turn his gaze away from me towards the clock. At the time I thought this was an indication that he was longing for the end of the session. A long time afterwards the patient reminded me of this dumb-show and gave me the explanation, reminding me that the youngest of the seven little kids found a hiding-place in the case of the wall-clock while his six brothers were gobbled up by the wolf. And so what he wanted to say was: Be kind to me. Must I be afraid of you? Are you going to gobble me up? Should I hide from you in the clock-case, like the youngest of the seven little kids?

The wolf whom he feared was undoubtedly the father, but his fear of the wolf was conditional upon its being in an upright position. His memory told him quite definitely that pictures of the wolf where he was on all fours or, as in the story of 'Little Red Riding Hood', lying in bed, did not frighten him. No less significant was the position that, according to our reconstruction of the primal scene, he had seen assumed by the female; this significance was restricted, however, to the sexual sphere. Once he had reached maturity the most striking phenomena in his erotic life were attacks of compulsive physical infatuation that occurred and disappeared again in mysterious succession, releasing enormous energy in him even at times where he was otherwise inhibited, and which were quite beyond his control. An especially valuable connection obliges me to delay a full evaluation of these compulsive love episodes a little longer, but I can state here that they were linked to a particular condition, hidden from his conscious mind, which we were first able to recognize during the therapy. The woman must have taken up the position attributed to his mother in the primal scene. From puberty onwards he felt a woman's greatest charm to be the possession of large, conspicuous buttocks; coitus in any position other than from behind gave him scarcely any pleasure at all. There is every justification, it is true, for the critical objection that a sexual preference of this kind for the rear parts of the body is a general characteristic of individuals inclined to obsessive-compulsive neurosis and that we are not justified in deriving this from any particular memory imprint from childhood. It is part of the structure of a disposition to anal eroticism and of the archaic features which distinguish such a constitution. Copulation from behind – 'more ferarum' [in the manner of beasts] – is after all certainly to be regarded as the phylogenetically older form. We shall return to this point, too, in later discussion, once we have noted down the material relating to his unconscious condition for sexual relations.

Let us now return to our discussion of the connections between the dream and the primal scene. According to our previous expectations, the dream should present the child, who is looking forward to having his wishes fulfilled on Christmas Day, with the image of sexual satisfaction received from his father, as seen in the primal scene, providing a model for the satisfaction which he himself longs to receive from his father. Instead of this image, however, there appears material from the story which his grandfather had told him a short time before: the tree, the wolves, the loss of the tail in the form of over-compensation, in the bushy tails of the creatures that are apparently wolves. A connection is missing, an associative bridge that would lead us from the content of the primal story to that of the wolf story. This connection is again provided by the position, and by the position alone. The tail-less wolf in the grandfather's story tells the others to *climb on top of him*. The memory of the image of the primal scene was awakened by means of this detail; in this way material from the primal scene could be represented by material from the wolf story and at the same time the number 2, denoting his parents, could be replaced in the desired manner by the larger number of wolves. The content of the dream underwent

45

a further transformation as the material from the wolf story adapted itself to the content of the tale of 'The Seven Little Kids', borrowing from here the number 7.

The transformation of the material – primal scene, wolf story, tale of 'The Seven Little Kids' – mirrors thought progression as the dream takes shape: longing for sexual satisfaction received from the father – understanding of the condition of castration attached to it – fear of the father. Only now, I think, have we arrived at a full explanation of the four-year-old boy's anxiety dream.

As to the pathogenic effect of the primal scene and the alteration in sexual development that its resurrection produced: after all we have already touched on, I shall be brief in my remarks. We shall only follow up the particular effect to which the dream gives expression. At a later stage, we must make it clear to ourselves that the primal scene does not give rise to a single sexual current, but to a whole series of them, a positive splintering of the libido. We must keep in view, moreover, the fact that the activation of this scene (I am deliberately avoiding the word 'memory' here) has the same effect as if it were a recent experience. The effectiveness of the scene has been postponed [*nachträglich*], and loses none of its freshness in the interval that has elapsed between the ages of 18 months and 4 years. In what follows we may perhaps find grounds for supposing that it had certain effects even at the time when it was witnessed, from the age of 18 months on.

When the patient submerged himself in the situation of the primal scene, he brought the following perceptions to light from his own experience: he had previously assumed that the process he had observed was an act of violence, but this did not accord with the expression of pleasure he saw on his mother's face; he had to acknowledge that what was at issue here was satisfaction. The essentially new fact that observation of his parents' intercourse brought him was the conviction that castration was a reality, a possibility which had already preoccupied his thoughts before then. (The sight of the two girls urinating, Nanja's threat, the governess's interpretation of the sticks of barley sugar, the memory of his father cutting a snake into pieces.) For now he could see with his own eyes the wound that Nanja had spoken of and understood that its presence was a condition of intercourse with his father. He could no longer confuse it, as he had done when watching the little girls, with the girls' bottoms.

The dream ended in fear, which was only allayed once he had his Nanja with him. He thus sought refuge from his father with her. His fear was a rejection of his wish for sexual satisfaction from his father, the aspiration that had implanted the dream. The expression of that fear – being gobbled up by the wolf – was simply the reversal – a regressive one, as we shall hear – of the wish for coitus with the father, that is, for satisfaction such as his mother had experienced. His latest sexual objective, the passive attitude towards his father, had succumbed to repression; fear of his father, in the form of the wolf-phobia, had taken its place.

And the force which drove this repression? All the facts of the case suggest that it could only be narcissistic genital libido, which, in the form of concern for his male member, resisted a satisfaction that appeared to be conditional upon the sacrifice of that member. He drew from his threatened narcissism the masculinity to defend himself against the passive attitude towards his father.

At this point in our account we recognize the need to modify our terminology. During his dream he had reached a new phase of sexual organization. Up until then the sexual opposites for him had been *active* and *passive*. Since the seduction, his sexual objective had been a passive one, that of having his genitals touched, which regression to the previous stage of anal-sadistic organization then transformed into the masochistic objective of being disciplined, punished. It was a matter of indifference to him whether he achieved this objective with a man or a woman. He had moved on from Nanja to his father regardless of the difference in sex, asking Nanja to touch his penis, hoping to provoke his father into beating him. In this way the genital aspect was disregarded; in his fantasy of being struck on the penis this connection, which had been concealed by regression, was able to find expression. But now the activation of the primal scene in his dream led him back to the genital mode of organization. He discovered the vagina and the biological meaning of male and female. He now understood that active equalled male, passive female. His passive sexual objective would have had to be transformed into a female one, expressed as being taken in intercourse by the father instead of having his father strike him on the penis or the bottom. This feminine objective now fell forfeit to repression, and had to be replaced by fear of the wolf.

Here, we must break off discussion of his sexual development until new light can be shed back on to this earlier stage from later stages of his history. In evaluating the wolf phobia we might add that his mother and father were both turned into wolves. His mother played the castrated wolf, which let the others climb on to its back, his father the wolf who did so. We have heard him say, however, that his fear related to the wolf only when it was in a standing position, that is, to the father. We are also struck by the fact that the fear in which the dream ends is foreshadowed in the grandfather's story. In that story the castrated wolf who let the others climb on to its back is overcome by anxiety as soon as he is reminded of the absence of his tail. It would seem, then, that during the dreaming process he identified with his castrated mother and is now struggling to resist this outcome. Translated, I hope accurately, it is as if he is saying: if you want to be satisfied by your father you must accept castration as your mother has done; but I do not want that. A distinct protest in favour of masculinity! Let us be clear, incidentally, that the great disadvantage of the sexual development in this particular case is that it is not an undisrupted one. It was first crucially influenced by the seduction and is now sent off course by the observation of coitus, the postponed effect of which is like a second seduction.

V
Some Matters for Discussion

The polar bear and the whale cannot wage war, so they say, because each is confined within his own element and is unable to make contact with the other. It is equally impossible for me to hold a discussion with workers in the field of psychology or neurosis who do not recognize the premises of psychoanalysis and regard its conclusions as mere artefacts. In the last few years, however, a further form of opposition has arisen, voiced by others who, in their own opinion at least, are practitioners of analysis, have no quarrel with its techniques and results, and simply consider themselves justified in drawing different conclusions from the same material and subjecting it to other interpretations.

Theoretical contradictions are for the most part fruitless, however. As soon as we begin to move away from the material that should be our source, we run the risk of becoming intoxicated by our own assertions, and we end up putting forward views that a moment's observation would have contradicted. It seems very much more to the purpose, then, to combat divergent views by testing them against individual cases and problems.

I have argued above that it would no doubt be considered improbable that 'at the tender age of 18 months a child should be capable of perceiving such a complicated event and retaining it so accurately in the unconscious;

second, that it is possible at the age of 4 to process the memory imprints received in this way, belatedly advancing to an understanding of what was seen; and finally, that the child should succeed by whatever method in making conscious the details of such a scene, witnessed and understood in such circumstances, in a way that is both coherent and convincing'.

This last question is purely a matter of fact. Anyone who takes the trouble to go to these kinds of depths in analysis, according to the techniques I have mapped out, will be readily convinced that it is indeed possible; those who do not do so, breaking off the analysis at some more superficial level, have renounced the right to pass judgement in this matter. But this does not settle the question of how we are to interpret what we encounter in depth analysis.

The two other reservations are based on a disparaging attitude towards impressions formed in early infancy, and a reluctance to ascribe such lasting effects to them. They prefer to seek the cause of neuroses almost exclusively in the serious conflicts of later life, and assume that the significance of childhood is simply a sham created in analysis by the neurotic's tendency to express present interests by means of involuntary memories and symbols drawn from his infant past. If we were to evaluate the significant moments of infancy in this way we would lose a great deal that goes to form the most intrinsic characteristics of analysis, as well as much, admittedly, that creates resistance to it and discourages outsiders from placing their trust in it.

Let us hold up for discussion, then, the view that scenes from early infancy such as are provided by the exhaustive analysis of neurotic individuals, of which the present case is an example, do not reproduce real events to which we may attribute some influence on the structuring of later life and on symptom formation, but are on the contrary fantasy-formations, drawing their inspiration from riper years, intended as a symbolic representation, so to speak, of real wishes and interests, and owing their emergence to a regressive tendency, a turning-away from the tasks of the present moment. If this is indeed the case, we need not bring such disconcerting expectations to bear on the inner life and the intellectual achievements of children still far from the age of discretion.

Quite apart from the wish to rationalize and simplify the difficult task, common to us all, there are various matters of fact that tend to support this view. At the very outset, moreover, one can clear up a particular misgiving that the practising analyst above all might harbour. It is true that if the interpretation of these scenes from infancy that we have put forward is the correct one, then nothing changes in the first instance in the way the analysis is carried out. If a neurotic individual does indeed have the unfortunate characteristic of turning his interest away from the present day in order to attach it to regressive fantasy substitute-formations of this kind, then there is nothing for it but to follow him along these paths and help him to bring these unconscious productions to consciousness for, leaving aside their lack of real value, they are extremely valuable to us as carriers and possessors in the present moment of the interest that we want to set free so that we can direct it towards the tasks of the present day. The analysis would have to follow exactly the same course as it would if, naively credulous, we took such fantasies for truth. The difference would be seen only at the end of the analysis, once these fantasies had been uncovered. One would then have to say to the patient: 'Good; the course taken by your neurosis has been as if, in your childhood years, you received memory imprints such as these and continued to weave stories around them. You realize, of course, that that is not possible. They were products of imaginative activity intended to divert you from the real-life tasks which confronted you. Now let us attempt to discover what these tasks were, and what connecting pathways existed between them and your fantasies.' It would be possible to implement a second phase of treatment, more closely concerned with real life, once these infantile fantasies had been dealt with.

To shorten this route, that is, to alter psychoanalytic therapy as it has been practised up to now, would be technically inadmissible. If we do not make the full extent of these fantasies conscious to the patient we cannot make available to him the interest that attaches to them. If we divert his attention from them as soon as we sense their existence and their general outlines, we are merely giving support to the work of repression that has rendered them inviolable, immune to the patient's best efforts. If we devalue them at too early a stage, perhaps by disclosing that we shall be dealing only with fantasies and that these are without any real significance, we shall never be able to enlist the patient's cooperation in leading them towards consciousness. Correctly practised, the analytic technique should remain unaltered, regardless of the value we ascribe to these scenes from infancy.

I have already mentioned that in interpreting these scenes as regressive fantasies one can appeal for support to a number of matters of fact. Above all to the fact that in therapy – in my experience to date – these scenes from infancy are not reproduced as memories but are the results of reconstruction. For many people, no doubt, this admission alone will appear to settle the dispute.

I do not wish to be misunderstood. Every analyst knows and has experienced on numerous occasions the way in which, when therapy has been successful, the patient will relate any number of spontaneous memories from childhood, and the physician will feel that he is completely innocent of the fact that they have surfaced – perhaps surfaced for the first time – since he has not suggested any content of this kind to the patient through some attempt at reconstruction. These previously unconscious memories do not even have to be true; they may be true, but their truth is often distorted and interspersed with fantasized elements in a very similar way to so-called cover-memories that have been spontaneously retained. I will say only that scenes such as we find in my patient's case, from such an early age and with such content, which then lay claim to such extraordinary significance for the history of the case, are not as a rule reproduced as memories but must be guessed at – reconstructed – from the sum total of indications, step by step and with considerable effort. This is sufficient for the purposes of my argument, whether I acknowledge that in cases of obsessive-compulsive neurosis such scenes are not conscious as memories, or whether I limit my remarks simply to the case which we are considering here.

Now I am not of the opinion that these scenes must necessarily be fantasies simply because they do not come back as memories. It seems to me that they are completely on a par with memory in that – as in the present case – they find a substitute in dreams, analysis of which regularly leads back to the same scene, reproducing every element of its content in tireless variation. To dream is, after all, to remember, even under the night-time conditions of dream-formation. It is through this recurrence in dreams that I would explain the fact that patients themselves gradually become firmly convinced of the reality of these primal scenes, with a conviction every bit as strong as that based on memory.

My opponents need not regard opposition to these arguments as a lost cause, and give up the fight. It is well known that dreams can be influenced. And the conviction of the analysand can be the outcome of suggestion, for which we are still seeking a role in the play of forces released in analytic treatment. A psychotherapist of the old school would suggest to his patient that he is healthy and has overcome his inhibitions, etc. etc.; the psychoanalyst, on the other hand, suggests that as a child he underwent this or that experience, which he must now recall in order to regain his health. Therein lies the difference between the two approaches.

Let us be clear that this last attempt at explanation on the part of my opponents amounts to a far more sweeping dismissal of scenes experienced in infancy than was first suggested. They were not to be realities, but fantasies. Now the demand is obviously that they should not be the patient's fantasies, but the analyst's, imposed on the analysand as a result of some personal complex or other. In response to this reproach the analyst will of course reassure himself by demonstrating how gradually the reconstruction of this fantasy – which he apparently implanted – came about, how, as it was built up, the process continued quite independently, on many counts, of any stimulus offered by the physician, how, from a certain phase of treatment onward, it appeared to be the point on which everything converged, and how, now that a synthesis has been achieved, the most diverse and remarkable results radiate out from it, how the problems and peculiarities of the patient's medical history, from the large to the very small, find their solution in this one single assumption; and he will assert that he does not see himself as possessing the astuteness necessary to concoct an event that could fulfil all these requirements at a single stroke. Even this plea, however, will have no effect on the part of the population that has not itself had the experience of analysis. Sophisticated self-deception, some will say; others: an absence of discernment; and no verdict will be reached.

We may now consider another factor that supports a hostile reading of these reconstructed scenes from infancy. It is as follows: all the processes which are brought into play in order to explain away these questionable formations as fantasies exist in reality and are to be acknowledged as significant. The averting of interest from the tasks of real life, the existence of fantasies as substitute-formations for actions that have not been performed, the regressive tendency expressed through these creations – regressive in more than one sense, inasmuch as there is a simultaneous shrinking back from life and a falling back on the past – this is all to the point and is regularly confirmed by analysis. We might well suppose that this would also be sufficient to account for what are apparently involuntary memories from early infancy such as we are discussing here, and according to the economic principles of scholarship this explanation is to be preferred over the other one, which cannot manage without bringing in new and unsympathetic assumptions.

I shall permit myself at this point to draw the reader's attention to the fact that the dissenting views to be found in current psychoanalytic literature are usually based on the principle of *pars pro toto*. From a whole which has been carefully pieced together and built up one removes just one or two of the effective factors, proclaims them to be the truth and denies the importance of the other parts and of the whole in favour of these. If we examine the group for which a preference is expressed, we find that it is the one containing material already familiar from elsewhere or whatever can most readily be connected with it. Thus for Jung we find it is actuality and regression, for Adler egoistic motives. The very things that are new about psychoanalysis and are most characteristic of it are the ones that are neglected, dismissed as a mistake. In this way the revolutionary advances of psychoanalysis, that uncomfortable notion, can most easily be repelled.

It is far from futile to emphasize that there was no need for Jung to present a single one of the factors that were invoked by the opposing point of view, to facilitate understanding of those scenes from childhood, as a new discovery. Present conflict, turning away from reality, substitute satisfaction in fantasy, regression to material from the past, all of this has always been an integral part of my own theories, similarly structured although perhaps with minor modifications in terminology. It was not the whole of it, but only the part concerned with causality, which permeates down from reality to the formation of neuroses in a regressive direction. Alongside this I left room for a second, *progressive* [progredient] influence, which works forward from childhood impressions, showing the way to the libido that shrinks back from life, and providing an explanation for that regression to childhood that would otherwise be incomprehensible. In my view, therefore, both these factors work together in symptom-formation, but an earlier instance of their working together seems to me equally significant. I would maintain that *childhood influence already makes itself felt in the initial situation of neurosis-formation, since its intervention is crucial in helping to determine whether, and at what point, the individual fails in his attempts to master the problems of real life.*

What is at issue, then, is the significance of the infantile factor. What is needed is to find a case that can prove its significance beyond all doubt. The case that is the subject of this detailed account is one such, since its distinguishing characteristic is the way in which neurosis in later life has been preceded by neurosis in the early years of childhood. It is for this very reason that I have chosen to write about this case. If anyone were to reject it on the grounds that animal phobia does not seem important enough to be regarded as an independent neurosis, let me point out that the phobia was immediately succeeded by compulsive ritual, and by compulsive actions and thoughts that will form the subject of the next section of this essay.

Neurotic illness in the fourth or fifth year of childhood proves most importantly that the experiences of infancy are enough in themselves to produce neurosis, and that it does not require flight from a task with which life confronts the individual. We might object that even the child constantly encounters tasks that he would perhaps like to evade. This is true, but it is easy to gain an overall sense of the life of a child before he starts school, and it is possible to investigate whether it contains a 'task' responsible for causing the neurosis. However, all that we discover are involuntary impulses [*Triebregungen*], which the child finds it impossible to satisfy and which he is not yet able to master, together with the sources from which they flow.

As we might expect, the tremendous shortening of the interval between the outbreak of the neurosis and the occurrence of the childhood experiences in question massively reduces the regressive element in the causation of neurosis, and gives us a clearer glimpse of the '*progressive*' element, the influence exercised by earlier impressions. The present case history will, I hope, provide a clear image of this relationship. For other reasons, too, childhood neurosis will provide a decisive answer to our question as to the nature of primal scenes and those earliest childhood experiences traced in analysis.

If we start from the uncontradicted premiss that we were technically correct in formulating a primal scene of this kind, and that a comprehensive solution to all the riddles posed by the complex of symptoms produced by that childhood illness demands that all the effects radiate out from it just as all the threads of analysis lead back to it, then as far as its content is concerned it is impossible that it could be anything but the reproduction of a reality experienced by the child. For the child, just like the adult, can only produce fantasies with material that he has acquired from somewhere; and the ways in which he might acquire it are in part closed to the child (reading, for example), while the period of time available for such acquisition is short and can easily be scrutinized for sources of this kind.

In our case, the primal scene contains the image of sexual intercourse between the child's parents in a position that is particularly favourable to observation of a certain kind. Now, it would give us no proof of the reality of this scene if we encountered it in a patient whose symptoms, that is, the effects of such a scene, had emerged some time in later life. Such a patient could have acquired impressions, ideas and knowledge at a wide variety of points in that long interval of time, which are then transformed into a fantasy image, projected back into his childhood and attached to his parents. But when the effects of such a scene emerge in the child's fourth or fifth year, he must have been present to witness it at an even earlier age. In that case, however, all the disconcerting conclusions remain in place that were produced by the analysis of infantile neurosis. Unless, of course, someone wished to conclude that the patient had not only unconsciously fantasized that primal scene, but had also dreamed up the change in his character, his fear of the wolf and his religious compulsion, an excuse, however, that is contradicted by his otherwise sober manner and the tradition of straightforwardness in his family. We must stick to our guns – there is nothing else for it – either the analysis based on his childhood neurosis is a delusion from start to finish, or else the way in which I have portrayed it above is the correct one.

We have already acknowledged ambiguity in the fact that the patient's predilection for the female 'nates' [buttocks] and for coitus in the position where these are particularly in evidence apparently invites connection with his observation of his parents' intercourse, whereas a preference of this kind is a general characteristic of those archaic constitutions that are disposed to obsessive-compulsive neurosis. There is a possible explanation to hand, namely that we resolve the contradiction as over-determination. The person whom he observed in this coital position was after all his very own father, from whom he might also have inherited the same constitutional predilection. Neither his father's later illness nor the family history are against it; as I have already mentioned, an uncle on his father's side died in a condition which must be construed as the last stage of a severe compulsive disorder.

In this context let us recall that when seducing the 3¼-year-old boy, his sister uttered a strange calumny against their dear old nurse, saying that she turned everyone upside down and took hold of their genitals. It is an unavoidable notion that at a similarly tender age his sister might have witnessed the same scene as her brother did later, and that this is where she derived the suggestion of people being turned upside down in the sexual act. Such an assumption would also indicate one possible source for her own sexual impetuosity.

[It was not my original intention to enter into any further discussion here of the real value of 'primal scenes', but since in the meantime I have been obliged to treat the topic in a broader context and without any polemical intention in my *Introductory Lectures on Psychoanalysis*, it would be misleading if I failed to apply to the present case points of view that I present there as decisive. In the interests of completeness and to correct any mistakes let me therefore add the following remarks: there is indeed another possible interpretation of the primal scene that forms the basis for my patient's dream, which diverts us a good way from the verdict that we reached earlier and relieves us of a number of difficulties. Admittedly, the theoretical approach, which seeks to reduce such scenes from infancy to mere regressive symbols, will not gain anything by this modification either; in fact it seems to me that this – or indeed any other – analysis of childhood neurosis puts an end to the matter once and for all.

In my opinion, it is also possible to interpret the facts of the case as follows: we cannot forgo our assumption that the child observes coitus and in doing so acquires the conviction that castration might be more than an empty threat; the significance adhering to the positions of man and woman, in the first place for the development of his fears, and subsequently as a condition of intercourse, leaves us no choice, moreover, but to conclude that it must have been 'coitus a tergo' [from behind], 'more ferarum' [in the manner of the beasts]. Another factor is less crucial, however, and could be left aside. The child might have observed coitus between animals, rather than between his parents, and then imputed it to his parents, as if he had decided that his parents would not do it any other way.

This interpretation is supported above all by the fact that the wolves in the dream are actually sheepdogs and appear as such in my patient's drawing. Shortly before the dream, the boy had repeatedly been taken to see the herds of sheep, and there he could have seen big white dogs like this and probably watched them copulating. I would also cite in this context the number 3 which the dreamer produced without any obvious motivation for doing so, and would assume that he retained a memory of the sheepdogs doing so on three occasions. On the night of his dream we find, in addition to expectant excitement, the transference on to his parents of *every detail* of the recently acquired memory-image; and it is only this that made possible those powerful emotional effects. There then came a belated understanding of those impressions received perhaps a few weeks or months before, a process which every one of us may perhaps have experienced for himself. Now, the transference from the copulating dogs to his parents was not brought about by a final stage in the procedure, which was dependent on words, but by seeking out the memory of a real scene where his parents were enjoying intimacy, which he could fuse with the situation of coitus. All the details of the scene that were claimed in the analysis of the dream might have been reproduced exactly. It really was a summer afternoon, during the time when the child was suffering from malaria, the parents were both present, dressed in white, as the child awoke from sleep, but – the scene was harmless. In his eagerness to learn, the remaining details were supplied later, on the basis of what he had learned from the dogs, by the child's wish to spy on his parents while they were making love, so that now the fantasy scene unfolded with all the effects we have attributed to it, just as if it had been entirely real and had not been glued together from two components, an earlier one without any real significance and a later one which had left a deep impression.

It is immediately apparent how much this eases the effort of credulity that we are called upon to make. We need no longer assume that the parents completed their act of coitus in the presence of their child, an idea that many of us find repugnant, even if he was indeed very small at the time. The part played by postponed response is considerably reduced, since it now applies only to a few months in the child's fourth year and does not draw at all on those first dim years of childhood. There is now almost nothing that might take us aback in the child's behaviour as he effects a transference from dogs to parents and replaces fear of the father with fear of the wolf. The child is, after all, at that stage of developing his view of the world that is characterized in *Totem and Taboo* as the return of totemism. The theory that seeks to explain the primal scene of neurosis as a retrospective fantasy that takes place in later life would appear to find considerable support in this observation, despite the fact that this particular neurotic individual is at the tender age of 4. Young as he is, he has succeeded in replacing an impression acquired at the age of 4 with a fantasized trauma occurring at the age of 18 months, a regression, however, that appears neither mysterious nor tendentious. The scene that he needed to produce had to fulfil certain conditions, which could only be found, precisely because of the circumstances of the dreamer's life, in this early time, such as the fact, for example, that his bed was in his parents' room.

Most readers will find what I can add here, drawing on the results of analysis in other cases, a decisive factor in making up their mind as to whether the interpretation I suggest is correct. It is not at all rare in the analysis of neurotic mortals to find that in very early childhood they have observed a scene – whether a real memory or a fantasy – in which the parents engage in sexual intercourse. It may perhaps be an equally frequent occurrence in individuals who do not go on to suffer from neurosis. It may perhaps form a regular part of their treasure chest of – conscious or unconscious – memories. Every time I was able to unravel such a scene through analysis, however, it demonstrated the same peculiarity that made us suspicious in the case of this particular patient, namely that it referred to 'coitus a tergo', the only position which makes an inspection of the genitals possible to the observer. We need surely doubt no longer that we are simply dealing with a fantasy that is perhaps regularly inspired by observation of the sexual intercourse of animals. Indeed, there is more: I indicated that my description of the 'primal scene' remained incomplete, since I was leaving it until later to relate the way in which the child disturbed his parents' act of intercourse. I must now add that the way in which this disturbance takes place is also the same in every case.

I can imagine that I have now made myself vulnerable to suspicions of a serious kind on the part of the reader of this case history. If I had these arguments in favour of such an interpretation of the 'primal scene' at my disposal, how could I begin to justify having first put forward a different view, one that was apparently so absurd? Or had I perhaps accumulated new evidence in the interval between writing the first draft of this case history and formulating the present additional material that obliged me to modify my original interpretation, and was yet unwilling for some reason to admit to this? Instead I shall make a different admission: it is my intention to close discussion as to the real value of the primal scene this time with a 'non liquet' [deferred judgement]. We have not yet reached the end of this case history, and in due course a moment will arise that will undermine the certainty that at present we believe we enjoy. Then there will be nothing for it but to refer the reader to those passages in my *Lectures* where I discuss the problem of primal fantasies, or primal scenes.]

VI
Obsessive-compulsive Neurosis

Now, for the third time, he was influenced in a way that decisively altered his development. At the age of 4½, when there was still no improvement in his state of irritability and anxiety, his mother decided to acquaint him with the stories of the Bible in the hope of distracting and uplifting him. She succeeded in doing so, for his introduction to religion put an end to the previous phase, but as a result the symptoms of anxiety were succeeded by symptoms of compulsive behaviour. He had previously found it difficult to fall asleep because he was afraid of having bad dreams such as he had had the night before Christmas; now, before he went to bed, he had to kiss every single holy picture in the room, recite prayers and make the sign of the Cross countless times over himself and the place where he slept.

An overall view suggests that his childhood can be divided into the following epochs: first, the period of pre-history lasting up until the seduction (at age 3¼) and including the primal scene; second, the period of altered character, lasting until the anxiety dream (at age 4); third, the period of animal phobia lasting until his introduction to religion (at age 4½); and after this the period of obsessive-compulsive neurosis, lasting until after his tenth year. That there should be a smooth transition at a given moment from one phase to the next is neither in the nature of things, nor in our patient's nature: it was characteristic of him, on the contrary, to hold on to what had gone before and to allow the most diverse currents to coexist. His difficult behaviour did not disappear when his anxiety appeared but continued, slowly diminishing, into his pious period. In this last phase, however, there is no further mention of the wolf phobia. The course of his obsessive-compulsive neurosis was discontinuous; the first attack was the longest and the most intense, with others occurring at the age of eight and ten, the cause each time being visibly connected with the content of the neurosis. His mother told him the sacred story herself and also made Nanja read it aloud to him from an illustrated book. The principal emphasis of their account fell naturally on the Passion narrative. Nanja, who was very pious and superstitious, provided her own commentary, but also had to listen to the objections and doubts expressed by the young critic. If the struggles which now began to shake him eventually concluded in the victory of faith this was not least as a result of Nanja's contribution.

What he claimed to remember of his reactions when introduced to religion met at first with definite incredulity on my part. These, I maintained, could not be the thoughts of a child of 4½ or 5; he was probably attributing to his early past ideas which had grown out of the reflections of an adult of nearly 30. But the patient would not hear of any such correction; I was unsuccessful in my attempts to win him over, as I had been able to do on many other occasions when we had differed in our judgements; eventually, in fact, I was obliged to believe him because of the coherence between his remembered thoughts and the symptoms he reported, as well as the way they fitted into his sexual development. I then told myself, moreover, that only a diminishing minority of adults can rise to a critique of religious doctrines such as this, a critique which I doubted this child to be capable of.

I shall now present the material which his memories supplied, and only afterwards shall I seek out the path which will lead us to understand it.

The impression that he received from narration of the sacred story, he told me, was not at first a pleasant one. He struggled to come to terms, first, with the suffering nature of the person of Christ, and then with the whole way in which his story fitted together. His dissatisfaction and criticism were directed towards God the Father. If he was omnipotent, it was his fault that people were bad and tormented other people, and then went to Hell for it. He should have made them good; he himself was responsible for everything evil and for all torments. He took exception to the commandment to offer the other cheek when someone strikes us, as he did to Christ's wish, when hanging on the Cross, that the cup should pass from him, but also to the fact that a miracle did not take place to prove that he was the Son of God. In this way his critical faculties were awakened and he was rigorous and unrelenting in sniffing out the weaknesses in the sacred narrative.

Rationalistic criticism was very quickly accompanied by brooding and doubts, which may reveal that secret impulses were also at work. One of the first questions he addressed to Nanja was whether Christ also had a backside. Nanja told him that he was a God, but also a man. As a man he had everything and did everything that other men did. He found this reply most unsatisfactory but comforted himself by saying that someone's bottom was just the continuation of their legs, after all. His fear of having to demean the sacred person of God, barely calmed by this, flared up again when the question surfaced in his mind as to whether Christ also shat. He did not dare put this question to the pious Nanja, but extricated himself in a way which she could not have bettered, by telling himself that since Christ made wine out of nothing, he could also make nothing out of food and was thus able to spare himself the need to defecate.

We shall come closer to understanding such brooding thoughts if we make the connection with an aspect of his sexual development that we discussed earlier. We know that since Nanja had rejected him and he had suppressed the beginnings of genital activity as a result, his sexual life had developed in the direction of sadism and masochism. He tormented and mistreated small creatures, and fantasized about beating horses; but on the other hand he also fantasized about the heir to the throne being beaten. In sadism he was able to maintain the ancient identification with his father, in masochism he had chosen that same father as his sexual object. He was thus right in the middle of a phase of pre-genital organization in which I perceive the disposition to obsessive-compulsive neurosis to lie. The gradual effect of the dream, which brought him under the influence of the primal scene, could have been to enable him to progress to the genital mode of organization, transforming his masochism towards his father into a feminine attitude towards him, into homosexuality. But the dream did not bring progress of this kind with it; it ended in fear. His relationship with his father, which should have led from the sexual object-ive of being punished by him to the next objective, that of being taken in sexual intercourse by his father, like a woman, was thrown back on to a more primitive level still by the protest of his narcissistic masculinity, and having been displaced on to a father-substitute was split off as fear of being gobbled up by the wolf, but was not by any means dealt with. Indeed, we can only do justice to these apparently complicated facts by maintaining our belief in the coexistence of three sexual aspirations, all focused on the father. From the time of the dream onwards he was unconsciously homosexual; during his neurosis he was at the level of cannibalism; the earlier masochistic attitude remained the dominant one. All three aspirations had passive sexual objectives; we find the same object and the same sexual impulse, but a split had occurred which caused them to evolve towards three different levels.

His knowledge of sacred history now gave him the opportunity to sublimate the dominant masochistic atti-tude towards his father. He became Christ, an identifica-tion that was facilitated, in particular, by the fact that they shared a birthday. This made him something great and also made him – though insufficient emphasis was put on the fact initially – a man. In his doubt as to whether Christ could have a backside we catch a glimmer of his repressed homosexual attitude, for the significance of this brooding thought can only be the question as to whether he can be used by his father as if he were a woman, as his mother was used in the primal scene.

When we come to the solution of other compulsive ideas we shall find confirmation of this interpretation. The repression of his passive homosexuality corresponds to his misgivings that it is insulting to make a connection between the sacred person of Christ and outrageous ideas of this kind. We might note that he made considerable efforts to keep this new sublimation clear of additional material drawn from the sources of repression. But he did not succeed in doing so.

We do not yet understand why he now also struggled to come to terms with the passive character of Christ and his ill-treatment at his father's hands, and thus also began to deny his previous masochistic ideal, even in its sublimated form. We can assume that this second conflict was particularly favourable to the emergence of humiliating compulsive thoughts from the first conflict (between the dominant masochistic current and the repressed homosexual one), for it is only natural that in inner conflict all counter-tendencies are added together, even if they come from the most diverse sources. New material that he related will allow us to discover the motive for his struggle and for his critical attitude towards religion.

His sexual exploration had also benefited from what he had been told of sacred history. Up until then, he had had no reason to assume that only women have children. On the contrary, Nanja had led him to believe that he was his father's child and his sister their mother's, and he had particularly valued this close relationship with his father. Now he learnt that Mary was called the Mother of God. So it was women who had children, and what Nanja said was no longer tenable. Furthermore, he was confused by the stories and was no longer sure who Christ's father was. He was inclined to think it was Joseph, since he had been told that they had always lived together, but Nanja said that Joseph was only *like* his father and that his real father was God. He could make nothing of this. All he understood was that, if it was possible to talk about it at all, the relationship between father and son was nothing like as intimate as he had always imagined it to be.

The boy sensed something of the ambivalence of feeling towards the father that is enshrined in all religions, and attacked his religion because it weakened that paternal relationship. Of course his opposition soon ceased to be doubt as to the truth of the doctrine and was instead turned directly against the person of God. God had been harsh and cruel in his treatment of his son, yet he behaved no better towards human beings. He had sacrificed his son and demanded the same of Abraham. He began to be afraid of God.

If he was Christ, then his father was God. But the God that religion sought to impose on him was no real substitute for the father he had loved and of whom he did not want to be deprived. His love for his father gave him his critical sharpness. He put up a fight against God so that he could hold on to his father, and in doing so was actually defending the old father against the new one. Here he had a difficult stage in the process of detaching himself from his father to complete.

Thus it was the old love for his father, revealed in earliest days, on which he drew for the energy to combat God and for the sharpness to criticize religion. On the other hand, this hostility towards the new God was not an original act but was modelled on a hostile impulse towards his father that had come into being under the influence of the anxiety-dream, and was fundamentally only the resurgence of the same impulse. The two opposing emotional impulses that were later to rule his whole life met here in a battle of ambivalence over the issue of religion. What this struggle yielded in the form of symptoms, his blasphemous ideas, the compulsion which came over him to think 'God – crud', 'God – swine' was also for this reason a genuine compromise outcome, as we shall see from the analysis of these ideas in the context of anal eroticism.

Some other compulsive symptoms of a less typical kind lead us with equal certainty to the father, but also reveal the connection between the obsessive-compulsive neurosis and the earlier chance occurrences.

One element in the ceremonial piety that he eventually used to expiate his blasphemies was the requirement that under certain conditions he should breathe in a ritual manner. When making the sign of the Cross he had to breathe in deeply each time or exhale loudly. In his language breath is the same as spirit. This, therefore, was the role of the Holy Spirit. He had either to breathe in the Holy Spirit or else to breathe out the evil spirits which he had heard and read about. He also ascribed to these evil spirits the blasphemous thoughts for which he imposed such great penance on himself. He was obliged to exhale, however, whenever he saw beggars, cripples, or ugly, old and wretched people, and he could not see how to connect this compulsion with the spirits. The only way he could account for it to himself was that he did it so as not to become like them.

Then, in connection with a dream, analysis brought the explanation that it was only after the age of five that he had begun to breathe out when he saw pitiful individuals, and that this was connected with his father. He had not seen his father for many long months when one day his mother said that she would take the children to the city and show them something that would make them very happy. She then took them to a sanatorium where they saw their father again; he looked ill and his son felt very sorry for him. His father, then, was the archetype of all those cripples, beggars and poor people, the sight of whom obliged him to breathe out, just as the father is normally the archetype of the grimaces seen in anxiety states and of the caricatures drawn to express contempt. We shall discover elsewhere that this pitying attitude goes back to a particular detail of the primal scene, which took effect at this late stage in the obsessive-compulsive neurosis.

The resolution not to become like them, which was the motivation for his breathing out in front of cripples, was thus the old identification with the father transformed into a negative. And yet he was also copying his father in a positive sense, for his noisy breathing was an imitation of the sounds he had heard his father make during intercourse. The Holy Spirit owed its origins to this sign of erotic excitement in a man. Repression turned this breathing into an evil spirit, for which there also existed a second genealogy, that of the malaria from which he had been suffering at the time of the primal scene.

The rejection of these evil spirits corresponded to an unmistakably ascetic aspect of his character, which was also expressed in other reactions. When he heard that Christ had once driven out evil spirits into pigs, which then plunged into an abyss, he thought of the way his sister, in the earliest years of her childhood, before he could remember, had rolled down from the harbour cliff-path on to the beach. She too was one of those evil spirits and pigs; it was only a short step from this to 'God – swine'. Even his father had turned out to be dominated by sensuality in just the same way. When he was told the story of the first man, he was struck by the similarity between Adam's fate and his own. He expressed hypocritical astonishment when talking to Nanja that Adam had allowed himself to be plunged into misery by a woman, and promised Nanja that he would never get married. Around this time, as a result of his sister's seduction, his feelings of enmity towards womankind found powerful expression. They were later to trouble him often enough in his erotic life. His sister became the permanent embodiment, to him, of temptation and sin. When he had been to confession he would feel pure and free from sin. But then it would seem as if his sister was watching for an opportunity to plunge him into sin once more, and before he was aware of it he would have provoked a quarrel with his sister, which made him sinful again. In this way he was obliged to reproduce the fact of seduction over and over again. He never, incidentally, divulged his blasphemous thoughts in the confessional, even though they weighed heavily on him.

We have unexpectedly progressed to a discussion of symptoms manifested in the later years of obsessive-compulsive neurosis; let us therefore skip the very great deal that occurred in the meantime and relate how the condition came to an end. We already know that, as well as being a permanent condition, it was subject to periodic intensification, such as on one occasion, which we are unable as yet to understand, when a boy in the same street died, with whom he was able to identify. When he was ten he acquired a German tutor who quickly came to have considerable influence over him. It is most instruct-ive to find that the whole heavy weight of piety disap-peared, never to return, once he had noticed, and learnt from his teacher's didactic conversation, that this father-substitute set no store by piety and did not believe in the truth of religion. His piety fell away, along with his dependence on his father, who was now being super-seded by a new, more affable father. It must be said that this did not occur without one last flaring-up of his obsessive-compulsive neurosis; he had a particularly strong memory of the compulsion to think of the Holy Trinity every time he saw three piles of dung lying together on the street. He simply never gave in to one stimulus without making a final attempt to keep hold of what no longer had any value for him. When his teacher talked him out of his cruelty towards small creatures he put a stop to his misdeeds, but not before he had had one last orgy of cutting up caterpillars. He behaved in exactly the same way in analytic treatment by developing a transi-tory 'negative reaction'; whenever something important had been resolved he would try to negate the effects for a while, in that there would be a worsening of symptoms that had been resolved. We know that in general children behave in a similar way in the face of prohibitions. When they have been told off, for example for making a disagreeable noise, they will repeat it once more after they have been told not to, before stopping. In doing so they make it look as if they have stopped voluntarily, thus defying the prohibition.

Under the German teacher's influence he found a new and better way to sublimate his sadism, which, as befitted his approaching puberty, had then gained the upper hand over his masochism. He developed a passion for military life, for uniforms, weapons and horses, and used this to feed his constant daydreaming. Under a man's influence he had thus got away from his passive attitudes and was initially on a fairly normal track. One after-effect of his attachment to his teacher, who left soon afterwards, was that in later life he preferred the German element (doctors, clinics, women) to the native one (representing the father), which was of great benefit for the therapeutic transference.

Another dream belongs in the period before his liberation by the teacher, which I mention here because it had been forgotten up until the moment when it surfaced in therapy. He saw himself riding a horse, pursued by a giant caterpillar. He recognized a reference here to a still earlier dream from the period before the teacher came, which we had interpreted long before. In this earlier dream he saw the devil in black robes, assuming the upright stance which had previously so terrified him in the wolf and the lion. With his outstretched finger he was pointing to a giant snail. He had quickly guessed that this devil was the demon who features in a well-known poem, and the dream itself a reworking of a widely disseminated picture showing the demon in a love-scene with a young girl. The snail, an exquisite symbol of female sexuality, stood for the woman. Guided by the demon's pointing gesture, we were quickly able to declare the meaning of the dream to be his longing for someone who could give him the final instruction he lacked in the mysteries of sexual intercourse, just as his father had first enlightened him long ago in the primal scene.

In amplification of the later dream, where the female symbol was replaced by the male one, he remembered a particular experience that had taken place a little while before. Riding on the estate one day he passed a peasant, asleep with his son lying next to him. The boy woke his father and said something to him, whereupon the father began to shout at the rider and ran after him, until he and his horse quickly moved off. This in conjunction with a second memory that on that same estate there were trees that were completely white, completely covered in caterpillar cocoons. We see that he took flight from realization of the fantasy that the son was sleeping with his father, and that he brought in the white trees to create a reference to the anxiety-dream, to the white wolves in the walnut tree. It was thus a positive eruption of fear expressed at the feminine attitude towards men, which initially he had defended himself against by means of religious sublimation; soon after that he was to defend himself against it even more effectively, by means of military sublimation.

It would be a major error, however, to assume that, once the compulsive symptoms had been eliminated, no permanent effects of the obsessive-compulsive neurosis remained. The process had led to the victory of pious belief over critical inquiry and rebellion, and was predicated upon repression of the homosexual attitude. Both factors resulted in permanent disadvantages. After this first great defeat his intellectual activity remained seriously impaired. He developed no particular eagerness to learn and demonstrated nothing of the critical acuity with which, at the tender age of five, he had subverted religious doctrine. The repression of his excessively strong homosexuality, which took place during the anxiety-dream, meant that this significant impulse was reserved for the unconscious mind, thus maintaining its original attitude towards its objective and eluding all the sublimations to which it would normally lend itself. For this reason, the patient lacked all the social interests which give content to life. Only as we succeeded through analytic therapy in releasing his homosexuality from its fetters was there a turn for the better in this state of affairs, and it was a remarkable thing to watch the way in which – without any urging on the part of the physician – each liberated element of his homosexual libido was eager to be brought to bear on life and attached to the great common concerns of humanity.

VII
Anal Eroticism and the Castration Complex

I must ask the reader to remember that this history of an infantile neurosis was recovered as a by-product, so to speak, of the analysis of a patient who had fallen ill in more mature years. I was thus obliged to piece it together out of even tinier fragments than those that are normally available when any kind of synthesis is attempted. Such work, which is otherwise not difficult, finds its natural limit at the point where it becomes a question of capturing a multidimensional structure in the two-dimensionality of description. I must therefore content myself with offering individual limbs which the reader can join together into a living whole. The obsessive-compulsive neurosis I have described developed, as I have emphasized repeatedly, out of an anal-sadistic constitution. Up until now, however, we have only considered one of these two principal factors, sadism and its transformations. Anything concerned with anal eroticism I have deliberately left on one side in order to give a full account of it here.

Analysts have long agreed that the many involuntary impulses [*Triebregungen*] that can be summed up as anal eroticism are extraordinarily and inestimably important to the development of the individual's sexual life and to inner activity as a whole. And equally, that one of the most important expressions of eroticism derived from this source and recast in a different mould is to be found in the treatment of money, a valuable substance which, in the course of the individual's life, attracts the psychic interest which properly belongs to that product of the anal zone, faeces. We have grown accustomed to tracing interest in money, where its nature is libidinal rather than rational, back to excremental pleasure, and to expect of any normal person that his relationship to money should be kept free of libidinal influences and controlled by realistic considerations.

In our patient's case this relationship was particularly badly disrupted at the time of his later illness, this being not the least important reason for his lack of independence and his inability to cope with life. Having inherited money from both his father and his uncle, he was now very rich and it was manifestly of great importance to him that people should know that he was a rich man; he could be greatly offended if he was underestimated in this regard. And yet he did not know how much he possessed, what his expenditure was, nor how much was left. It was difficult to know whether to call him a miser or a spendthrift. Sometimes he behaved one way, sometimes another, but never in a way that suggested consistent intentions. Certain striking traits of character, which I shall describe later, might lead one to conclude that he was an unrepentant swank who regarded his wealth as his greatest personal asset and who would never even begin to put feelings on a par with money. But he did not judge other people according to their wealth and there were many occasions when he actually turned out to be modest, sympathetic and ready to help. It was simply that money eluded his conscious control and held another meaning for him.

I mentioned earlier that I regarded with deep suspicion the way in which he consoled himself for the loss of his sister – who in the later years of her life had become his best friend – with the thought that now he would not need to share their parents' inheritance with her. More striking still, perhaps, was the calm way in which he could tell me this, as if he had no comprehension of the coarseness of feeling to which he was admitting. Analysis rehabilitated him to some extent by demonstrating that his pain at his sister's death had merely been displaced, but now it seemed more incomprehensible than ever that he should have thought he could find a substitute for his sister in his increased wealth.

His behaviour in another instance seemed to be a mystery even to him. After his father's death, the fortune he had left was divided between himself and his mother. It was administered by his mother, who responded to his requests for money, as he himself acknowledged, with irreproachable generosity. And yet any discussion of money matters between them would end with the most violent reproaches on his part: that she did not love him, that her only thought was to save money by keeping him short, and that she would probably prefer it if he were dead, so that she could have all the money for herself. In tears his mother would then protest her unselfish motives and he would be ashamed, assuring her quite truthfully that he really did not think of her in that way, and yet sure that the same scene would be repeated on the next occasion.

That faeces signified money to him long before he entered analysis can be seen from many chance occurrences, two of which I shall relate here. At a time when his bowels were still unconnected with his illness, he once visited a poor cousin living in a large town. As he left he reproached himself for not giving his cousin financial support, whereupon he immediately had 'perhaps the strongest urge to defecate he had ever felt in his life'. Two years later he did indeed offer to pay his cousin an allowance. And the other instance: at the age of 18, while preparing for his final examinations at school, he visited a fellow-student and came to an agreement with him which seemed advisable in the light of the fear they both felt of failing the examination. They had decided to bribe the school janitor, and his share of the money they needed to find was of course the larger one. On the way home he was thinking that he would willingly pay even more if he could only pass, if only nothing would go wrong in the examination, and he did indeed have a little accident before he could reach his own front door.

All this prepares us for the fact that during his later illness he suffered from extremely persistent disturbance of the bowel function, though one that fluctuated with different causes. When he entered treatment with me he had become accustomed to receiving enemas, administered by a companion; he might not experience spontaneous emptying of the bowels for months at a time, unless there was sudden stimulus from a particular quarter, following which normal bowel activity would be resumed for a few days. His principal complaint was that he felt the world to be shrouded in a veil, or that there was a veil dividing him from the world. This veil was torn open only at the moment when the content of the bowel left the bowel after an enema, whereupon he would feel healthy again, and normal.

The colleague to whom I referred my patient for an assessment of his bowel condition was sufficiently perceptive to declare it to be determined by functional or even psychic factors, and to eschew medical intervention. Neither this, incidentally, nor the diet he ordered my patient to follow were of any use. During the years in which he was in analysis he never had any spontaneous bowel movements (except under the influence of those sudden stimuli). The patient allowed himself to be persuaded that any more intensive treatment of the refractory organ would simply make the condition worse, and was content to bring about a forced evacuation of the bowels once or twice a week by means of an enema or laxative.

In discussing these disruptions to the function of the bowel I have allowed my patient's later state of illness to take up more space than I had intended in a piece of work devoted to his childhood neurosis. There were two reasons for my decision: first, the fact that the bowel symptoms had remained virtually unchanged from the period of childhood neurosis to the later one, and, second, that they were enormously significant in bringing the treatment to an end.

We know how important doubt is to the physician analysing a case of obsessive-compulsive neurosis. It is the patient's most powerful weapon, his preferred means of resistance. For years, thanks to this doubt, our patient too was able to let the efforts made in therapy bounce off him, safe behind a barricade of respectful indifference. Nothing changed, and there was no way of convincing him. Finally I recognized the significance of his bowel disorder for my intentions: it represented the touch of hysteria that is regularly found to underlie any obsessive-compulsive neurosis. I promised the patient that his bowel activity would be fully restored; my undertaking forced his disbelief into the open, so that I then had the satisfaction of watching his doubt disappear as his bowel began to 'add its voice' to the work, as if it were an hysterically affected organ, regaining its normal function, which had for so long been impaired, in the course of a few weeks.

I shall now return to the patient's childhood, to a time when faeces cannot possibly have signified money to him.

He experienced bowel disorders at a very early age, especially the most common kind, entirely normal in children, namely incontinence. We would undoubtedly be correct, however, in rejecting any kind of pathological explanation for these earliest incidents and seeing in them merely proof of his intention not to be disturbed in or held back from the pleasure accompanying the function of evacuation. He continued to be greatly amused, well into his later illness, by anal jokes and exhibitions of the kind that appeal to the natural coarseness of many sections of society.

During the era of the English governess it repeatedly came about that he and Nanja were obliged to share a bedroom with the woman they loathed. Nanja noted sympathetically that it was always on these nights that he soiled the sheets, something that he normally no longer did. He was not at all ashamed of this: it was an expression of his defiance towards the governess.

A year later (at the age of 4½), during his period of great anxiety, it so happened that he once soiled his trousers during the day. He was dreadfully ashamed, wailing as he was cleaned up that he could not go on living like this. Something had changed in the meantime, then, and by turning our attention to his lament we can track down what it was. It turned out that the words 'he could not go on living like this' were spoken in imitation of someone else. On some occasion or other his mother had taken him along when she accompanied to the railway station the doctor who had come to visit her. As they walked she was lamenting her pains and bleeding and exclaimed, in those selfsame words, 'I cannot go on living like this', without imagining that the child whose hand she was holding would retain them in his memory. The lament, which he was incidentally to repeat on countless occasions in his later illness, thus signified his identification with his mother.

Soon a missing link between the two incidents, as regards both time and content, came into his memory. Once, at the beginning of his period of anxiety, it came about that his mother, greatly concerned, issued warnings that the children were to be guarded against the dysentery that had made an appearance in the vicinity of their estate. He inquired what that might be and, when he heard that one symptom of dysentery is blood in the stools, he became very anxious and claimed to have found blood in his own stools; he was afraid of dying of dysentery, but allowed himself to be examined and persuaded that he had made a mistake and that there was no need to be afraid. We can understand that his anxiety was an attempt to carry through the identification with his mother, about whose bleeding he had heard in the conversation with the doctor. In his later attempt to identify with his mother (at the age of 4½) he had dispensed with the blood; he no longer understood what it was he was feeling, thought that he was ashamed of himself and did not know that he was seized with mortal fear; yet this is what his lament quite unambiguously reveals.

At that time his mother, suffering as she did from gynaecological complaints, was generally fearful for herself and her children, and it is perfectly probable that his anxiety was founded on identification with his mother, as well as the other motives which fuelled it.

Now, what is the significance of his identification with his mother?

Between his impudent exploitation of incontinence at the age of 3½ and his horror of it at the age of 4½ there lies the dream that inaugurated the period of anxiety, bringing a belated understanding of the scene he experienced at the age of 18 months and enlightenment as to a woman's role in the sexual act. The obvious explanation is that the change in his attitude towards defecation is also connected with that great upheaval. Dysentery was clearly the name of the illness he had heard his mother complaining about, the one you could not go on living with; his understanding was that his mother's illness was not gynaecological in nature, but an illness of the bowel. Under the influence of the primal scene he inferred that the connection ran as follows: his mother's illness was due to the thing his father had done with her, and his fear of finding blood in his stools, that is, of being as ill as his mother, was the rejection of his identification with his mother in that sexual scene, the same rejection that awakened him from his dream. His fear was also proof, however, that in his later processing of the primal scene he had put himself in his mother's place and envied her this relationship with his father. The organ through which he could express his identification with the female and his passive homosexual attitude towards the male was the anal zone. Dysfunction in this zone had acquired the significance of the stirrings of feminine tenderness, which it retained also during his later illness.

At this point we must air an objection, discussion of which could contribute greatly to clarification of an apparently confused state of affairs. We have had to assume that during the dreaming process he understood women to be castrated, having a wound in the place of the male member which serves the purposes of sexual intercourse, and that castration was thus the condition of female identity; under the threat of this loss he repressed the feminine attitude towards the male and awoke in fear from his homosexual raptures. How is this understanding of sexual intercourse, this acknowledgement of the vagina, to be reconciled with his choice of the bowel as a means of identification with the female? Are his bowel symptoms not founded on what is probably a more ancient conception, which entirely contradicts castration anxiety, that of the anus as the site of sexual intercourse?

It is true that this contradiction exists and that the two

conceptions are inconsistent with one another. The question is merely whether they need to be consistent. We are disconcerted because we are always inclined to treat unconscious inner processes as if they were conscious ones, forgetting the profound differences between the two psychic systems.

When in excited anticipation the Christmas dream conjured up the image of his parents' sexual intercourse, once observed (or reconstructed), the old view of it no doubt occurred to him first, according to which that part of the woman's body receiving the penis was the anus. What else could he have thought when he watched this scene at the age of 18 months? But now, at the age of 4, came the new event. His previous experiences, the hints he had received as to the possibility of castration, now awoke and cast doubt on his 'cloaca theory', prompting recognition of the difference between the sexes and the sexual role of the female. He then behaved as children generally do when they are given an explanation they do not want – whether of sexual matters or of anything else. He rejected the new one – in this case, motivated by castration anxiety – and held on to the old one. He decided in favour of the bowel and against the vagina in the same way as he did later, and for similar motives, when he took his father's part against God. The new explanation was rejected, and he held fast to the old theory, which probably provided the material for his identification with the female, later appearing as the fear of a death brought on by bowel infection, and for his first religious scruples, such as whether Christ had a backside. Yet it is not as if his new insight had failed to have any effect; on the contrary, it took effect in a remarkably powerful way, providing the motivation for keeping the whole dream process in a state of repression and excluding it from later, conscious assimilation. But this was the full extent of the effect it had, for it had no influence in deciding the sexual problem. It was indeed a contradiction that, from that point onward, castration anxiety could exist alongside identification with the female by means of the bowel, but it was only a logical contradiction, which does not mean very much. Rather, the whole process is characteristic of the workings of the unconscious. Repression is a different thing from out-of-hand dismissal.

In studying the genesis of the wolf phobia we were tracing the effects of the new insight into the sexual act; now, investigating disorderly bowel activity, we find ourselves in the realm of the ancient cloaca theory. The two standpoints remain separated from each other by a stage of repression. The female attitude towards the male, dismissed through the act of repression, withdraws, so to speak, into bowel symptoms and expresses itself through the frequent episodes of diarrhoea, constipation and bowel pain of the patient's childhood years. His later sexual fantasies, constructed on the basis of correct sexual knowledge, can now be expressed regressively as bowel disorder. We cannot understand them, however, until we have uncovered the change in meaning that faeces have undergone since the patient's earliest childhood.

I hinted earlier that I had kept back a part of the content of the primal scene, which I can now fill in. The child eventually interrupted his parents' intimacy by evacuating his bowels, thus providing a motive for his crying. As far as criticism of this additional information is concerned, the same holds true here as for my previous discussion of the content of this scene. The patient accepted this reconstructed concluding action and appeared to confirm it by means of 'transitory symptoms'. A further additional detail that I had suggested, namely that the father had been annoyed by the disturbance and given vent to his displeasure by shouting at the child, had to be dropped. There was no reaction to it in the material of the analysis.

The detail which I have just supplied is not, of course, all of a piece with the rest of the scene's content. Here it is not a question of something imprinted on the memory from outside, which we can expect to encounter again in any number of later indications, but rather of the child's own reaction. Not a single detail of the story would change if this manifestation had not occurred, or if it had been inserted into the sequence of events later on. There is no doubt as to how we are to understand it, however. It signifies excitement in the anal zone (in the broadest sense of the word). In other cases of a similar type the observation of sexual intercourse ended in urination; in the same circumstances an adult male would be aware of an erection. The fact that the little boy produces a stool as a sign of his sexual excitement is to be judged as characteristic of the sexual constitution that is already in place. He immediately takes up a passive attitude and shows a greater inclination towards later identification with the female than with the male.

Here he uses the contents of the bowels in the same way as any other child, in one of its first and earliest senses. Faeces are the first *gift*, the child's first loving sacrifice, a part of his own body that is relinquished, but only in favour of a beloved person. Its use as an act of defiance, as in this case towards the governess at the age of 3½, is merely to give its earlier meaning as a gift a negative slant. The 'grumus merdae' left by burglars at the scene of the crime appears to have both meanings: both scorn and a regressive way of offering compensation. When a higher level has been reached, the earlier one can always be put to use in a negative, debased sense. Repression finds expression in the coexistence of antithetical impulses.

At a later stage of sexual development, faeces assume the meaning of *babies*. Babies are born through the anus, after all, just like stools. The meaning of faeces as a gift readily permits this transformation. Linguistic usage refers to babies as 'gifts'; we hear more frequently of the woman 'presenting her husband with a baby', but in unconscious usage equal weight is quite rightly given to the other side of the relationship, with the woman 'receiving' the baby from her husband as a gift.

The meaning of faeces as money arises from its meaning as a gift, but branches off in another direction.

The deeper meaning behind our patient's early covermemory of producing his first tantrum because he did not get enough Christmas presents is now revealed. What was missing was sexual satisfaction, which he had taken in an anal sense. His sexual exploration before the dream had prepared him for the fact, grasped during the dreaming process, that the sexual act solves the mystery of where babies come from. Even before the dream he did not like tiny children. Once he found a little bird, still naked, which had fallen out of the nest and, taking it for a tiny human being, had been filled with dread. Analysis demonstrated that all the tiny creatures, caterpillars and insects he had raged against had signified tiny children in his mind. His own relationship with his elder sister had given him cause to think a great deal about how older children relate to younger ones; and when on one occasion Nanja told him that his mother loved him so much because he was the youngest he acquired an understandable motive for wishing that there should be no younger child to follow him. His fear of this youngest child was then re-activated under the influence of the dream that brought his parents' intercourse to his attention.

We ought therefore to add a new sexual current to those we already know about; like the others it stems from the primal scene reproduced in the dream. In his identification with the female (the mother) he is ready to give his father a child and is jealous of the mother who has already done so, and may perhaps do so again.

By way of this detour demonstrating a common point of departure in their significance as gifts, money can now attract to itself the meaning of children, and in this way take over the expression of feminine (homosexual) satisfaction. In our patient's case this process occurred once at a time when brother and sister were both staying in a German sanatorium, and he saw his father give his sister two large banknotes. In fantasy he had always harboured suspicions about his father and his sister; now his jealousy was awakened and he fell on his sister as soon as they were alone, demanding his share of the money with such violence and heaping such reproaches on her that his sister, weeping, threw the whole amount at him. It was not just the real matter of the money that had upset him, but rather the baby, the anal sexual satisfaction he desired from his father. This, then, was his source of comfort when his sister died – during their father's lifetime. The scandalous thought which occurred to him when he heard the news of her death in fact meant simply: now I am the only child and my father must love me and me alone. Yet while the thought in itself was entirely capable of becoming conscious, its homosexual background was so unbearable that it was easier to disguise it as filthy greed, for this no doubt came as a great relief.

It was the same story when, after his father's death, he reproached his mother so unjustly for wanting to cheat him out of his money, for loving money more than she loved him. His old jealous feelings that she might love a child other than himself, and the possibility that she might have hoped for another child after him, compelled him to make accusations which he himself acknowledged to be groundless.

This analysis of the meaning of faeces makes it clear that the compulsive thoughts obliging him to make a connection between God and faeces had another meaning besides the abuse he thought them to be. They were in fact a true compromise outcome in which a current of tender devotion played just as much of a part as that of hostile invective. 'God – crud' was probably an abbreviated form of an offer which sometimes comes to one's ears in unabbreviated form. 'To shit on God' or 'to give a shit for God' can also mean to give him a baby, to be presented by him with a baby. The old meaning of 'gift', negatively debased, and the meaning of 'baby' which later developed out of this are combined in the patient's compulsive phrase. The latter expresses a feminine tenderness, a readiness to renounce manliness if in return one can be loved as a woman. Precisely that impulse towards God, then, articulated so unambiguously in the delusive system devised by the paranoid president of the Senate, Schreber.

When, later, I come to describe the resolution of the patient's last symptoms, we shall see once again how his bowel disorder had placed itself at the service of the homosexual current, expressing the feminine attitude towards the father. A new meaning of faeces will now clear the ground for a discussion of the castration complex.

Given that the column of faeces stimulates the erogenous mucous membrane of the bowel, it functions as an active organ, behaving as the penis does towards the mucous membrane of the vagina and acting as a precursor of the penis, so to speak, in the cloacal phase. The surrender of faeces in favour of (out of love for) another person, for its part, becomes the model of castration and is the first case in which a part of one's own body is renounced in the hope of winning favour from a beloved other. What is otherwise narcissistic love for one's own penis is thus not without some trace of anal eroticism. And so faeces, baby, penis, all come together to form a single entity, one unconscious concept – 'sit venia verbo' ['if you will excuse the expression'] – that of something small that can be separated from the body. Along these connecting pathways displacements and reinforcements of libido-charge [*Libidobesetzung*] can take place that are significant to a patient's pathology and can be uncovered in analysis.

We now know what our patient's initial attitude towards the problem of castration was. He dismissed it out of hand, maintaining that intercourse took place in the anus. When I say 'dismissed', I mean by this primarily that he refused to know anything about it, in the sense of repressing it. He did not actually pass judgement as to whether it existed or not, but effectively it did not. This attitude cannot have remained the definitive one, however, even during the years of childhood neurosis. Later on we can produce good evidence to show that he acknowledged castration as a fact. On this point, too, he behaved in that characteristic way that certainly makes both description and empathetic response so extraordinarily difficult. At first he expressed resistance, then gave in, but the one reaction did not cancel out the other. In the end two contradictory currents existed alongside one another, one of which abhorred the very idea of castration, while the other was prepared to accept it, consoling itself with femaleness as a substitute. The third current, the oldest and deepest, which had simply dismissed castration out of hand, without entertaining even the possibility of judging whether it was real or not, could no doubt also still be activated. Elsewhere I have recounted an hallucination that occurred to this selfsame patient at the age of five, which in this context requires only the addition of a short commentary:

'When I was five I was playing in the garden near my nurse, using my penknife to carve the bark of one of those walnut trees which also came up in my dream.

Suddenly I was inexpressibly terrified to discover that I had cut right through the little finger of my (right or left?) hand, so that it was only attached by the skin. I felt no pain, only great fear. I did not dare say anything to my nurse, who was only a few steps away, but sank down on to the nearest bench and just sat there, incapable of even glancing at my finger. In the end I calmed down, took a long look at my finger and, lo and behold, it wasn't damaged at all.'

We know that after he had been introduced to sacred history at the age of 4½, intense intellectual activity set in, which later turned into compulsive piety. We may therefore assume that this hallucination occurred around the time when he was making up his mind to acknowledge the reality of castration, and that it was perhaps intended to mark precisely that step. Even the patient's little correction is not without interest. If he hallucinated the same horrific experience which Tasso relates of his hero Tancred in 'Jerusalem Liberated', we are justified in suggesting that, for my young patient too, the tree represented a woman. He was thus playing the role of the father, bringing together his mother's bleeding, which he knew about, and the castration of women, the 'wound', which he now acknowledged.

The stimulus to hallucinate about cutting off a finger was provided, he told me later, by the story of one of his relatives who was born with six toes, the superfluous member being hacked off immediately with an axe. Thus women had no penis because it had been removed at birth. In this way he came to accept, at the time when he was suffering from obsessive-compulsive neurosis, what he had learned in the dream process and rejected at that time by means of repression. The ritual circumcision of Christ, and of the Jews in general, could not, moreover, have remained unknown to him at a time when he was reading and discussing the sacred story.

It was undoubtedly at this time that his father became the terrifying figure who threatens castration. The cruel God with whom he was wrestling, who allowed people to become guilty so that he could then punish them, who sacrificed his own son and the sons of men, threw the shadow of his character back on to the father – whom the boy sought to defend, on the other hand, against that same God. He has a phylogenetic schema to fulfil here and manages to do so even though his own personal experiences do not seem to square with it. The threats, or hints, of castration he had received had actually emanated from women, but this did not delay the end result for long. In the end it was his father at whose hands he feared castration. On this point heredity triumphed over accidental experience; in the pre-history of the human race it was certainly the father who carried out castration as a punishment, subsequently reducing it to the practice of circumcision. The more he repressed his sensuality as the process of obsessive-compulsive neurosis went on, the more natural it seemed to him to endow his father, that true representative of sensual activity, with evil intentions of this kind.

The identification of his father with the castrator was significant in that it was the source of an intense uncon-scious hostility towards him – which went as far as wishing him dead – as well as of the guilt he felt in response to this. To this extent he was, however, behaving normally, that is, like any other neurotic individual possessed by a positive Oedipal complex. What was remarkable was that in him a counter-current existed for this too, according to which his father was in fact the castrated figure, and as such demanded his sympathy.

In my analysis of the breathing rituals prompted by the sight of cripples, beggars, etc., I was able to show that this symptom could also be traced back to the father, whom he had felt sorry for when he visited him in the clinic during his illness. Analysis permitted us to trace this thread back still further. Very early on, probably even before the seduction (at the age of 3¼), there was a poor day-labourer on the estate whose job it was to carry water into the house. He was unable to speak, supposedly because his tongue had been cut out. He was probably a deaf mute. The little boy was very fond of him and pitied him with all his heart. When he died, he looked for him in the heavens. This man was thus the first of the cripples for whom he felt such sympathy and, judging by the context and the point at which he was mentioned in analysis, undoubtedly a father-substitute.

In analysis other memories followed on from this of servants whom he liked; in each case he dwelt on the fact that they were in poor health or Jewish (circumcision!). The lackey who helped clean him up after his little accident at the age of 4½ was Jewish, too, as well as consumptive, and enjoyed his sympathy. All these figures can be placed in the period before he visited his father in the sanatorium, that is, before formation of the symptom, which was really intended to keep identification with the person pitied at a distance by means of exhalation. Then suddenly, in connection with a dream, the analysis turned back to the patient's very early life, giving him the opportunity to assert that he had observed the disappearance of the penis in coitus during the primal scene, pitied his father on this account and rejoiced at the reappearance of what he had thought to be lost. Another new feeling, then, inspired by this scene. Incidentally, we cannot fail to recognize the narcissistic roots of such sympathy, underlined by the word itself.

VIII
Supplementary Material from Earliest Childhood – Solution

It is often the case in analysis that new material surfaces in the memory once the end is in sight, material which up until then has been kept carefully hidden. Or else an inconspicuous remark will be tossed casually into the conversation, in an indifferent tone of voice, as if it were something quite superfluous, and then something else added on another occasion which makes the physician prick up his ears, until we finally recognize that these passed-over scraps of memory hold the key to the most important of secrets, glossed over by the patient's neurosis.

At an early stage my patient had recounted a memory dating from the time when his difficult behaviour would suddenly veer over into anxiety. He was chasing a lovely big butterfly with yellow stripes, whose large wings had pointed tips – a swallow-tail, in fact. Suddenly, as the butterfly settled on a flower, he was overcome by a terrible fear of the creature and ran away screaming.

This memory recurred from time to time in the analysis and demanded some sort of explanation, which for a long time was not forthcoming. We could assume from the outset that a detail of this kind had not retained a place in his memory for its own sake, but was a cover-memory representing something more important which was somehow bound up with it. One day he said that in his language the word for a butterfly was Babuschka, or little granny; butterflies in general made him think of women and girls, while beetles and caterpillars were like boys. It must surely have been the memory of a female, then, which had been awakened in that scene of anxiety. I will not conceal the fact that at the time I suggested as a possibility that the yellow stripes of the butterfly reminded him of similar stripes on an item of clothing worn by a woman. I do so only in order to show by example how inadequate the physician's conjectures are as a general rule in solving questions that have been raised, and how wrong it is to attribute responsibility for the outcome of the analysis to the physician's fantasies and suggestions.

Many months later, in an entirely different context, the patient remarked that it was the way the butterfly's wings opened and closed once it had settled that had given him such an uncanny feeling. It had been like a woman opening her legs, and the legs then made the shape of a Roman V, which as we know was the hour at which he used to experience a darkening of his mood, both in his boyhood and in the present day.

This was a notion that would never have occurred to me and that I was the more inclined to value when I considered that the process of association it revealed was genuinely infantile in character. I have often noticed that a child's attention is drawn by movement far more often than by forms that are at rest, and he will often produce associations on the grounds of a similar kind of movement, which we adults neglect to notice or overlook altogether.

For a long time afterwards this little problem was left on one side. I will mention only the commonplace conjecture that the butterfly's pointed, protruding wing tips might have had some significance as genital symbols.

One day a memory of a kind came to the surface, hazy and diffident: very early on, even before the time of his nurse, he must have had a nursery-maid who was very fond of him. She had had the same name as his mother. He was sure he had returned her affection. A first love, then, which had vanished without trace. We agreed, however, that something must have happened then that was to be of importance later.

Then he revised his memory once more. She could not have had the same name as his mother, that was a mistake on his part, proving of course that in his memory she had merged with his mother. Her real name had come back to him by a circuitous route. He suddenly found himself thinking of a store-room on the first estate where fruit was kept after it had been picked, and of a particular sort of pear with an excellent flavour, a large pear with yellow-striped skin. In his language the word for pear was 'Gruscha', and this had also been the name of the nursery-maid.

It thus became clear that behind the cover-memory of the butterfly he had chased there lay concealed the memory of this nursery-maid. The yellow stripes were not on her dress, however, but on the pear whose name she shared. Yet where did his anxiety come from when this memory was activated? The most obvious, crass conjecture might have been that as a small child it was this nursery-maid whom he had first seen perform movements of the legs which he had fixed in his mind with the Roman symbol V, movements which allowed access to the genitals. We spared ourselves such conjectures and waited for new material to emerge.

Soon afterwards came the memory of a scene, incomplete but, as far as it went, distinct. Gruscha was kneeling on the ground, beside her a pail and a short broom made of birch twigs tied together; he was there and she was teasing him or scolding him.

We could easily supply the missing information from elsewhere. In the first months of therapy he had told me about his compulsive infatuation with a peasant girl from whom at the age of 18 he had caught the infection which led to his later illness. At the time he had been conspicuously unwilling to give the girl's name. It was an isolated instance of resistance; normally he gave unqualified obedience to the ground rules of analysis. He claimed, however, that he was so very ashamed to say the name out loud because it could only belong to a peasant; a girl of better breeding would never have been given such a name. Eventually we learned that this name was *Matrona*. It had a motherly ring to it. His shame was obviously displaced. He was not ashamed of the fact that he felt these infatuations exclusively for girls of the most lowly birth, he was ashamed only of the name. If the affair with Matrona had anything in common with the Gruscha episode, then we could locate his feelings of shame back in that earlier incident.

On another occasion he told me how very moved he was when he heard the story of Johannes Huss; his attention was caught by the bundles of twigs that were dragged to the place where he was burned at the stake. His sympathy for Huss awoke a particular suspicion in me; I have often encountered it in younger patients and have always found the same explanation to hold true. One of them had even produced a dramatic version of Huss's story; he began to write his drama on the very day the object of his secret infatuation was taken away from him. Huss is burnt to death, and, like others who fulfil the same condition, he is a hero to those who formerly suffered from enuresis. The patient himself made a connection between the bundles of twigs around Huss's funeral pyre and the nursery-maid's broom (made of birch twigs).

This material fitted together effortlessly to fill in the gaps in his memory of the scene with Gruscha. As he was watching the girl cleaning the floor he had urinated into the room; at this she had threatened him, no doubt playfully, with castration. I do not know if my readers are already able to guess why I have described this episode from early infancy in such detail. It establishes an important link between the primal scene and the compulsive eroticism that was later to have such a decisive effect on his fortunes, and introduces, moreover, a sexual condition which throws some light on that compulsion.

When he saw the girl crouched down cleaning the floor, on her knees with her buttocks projecting and her back horizontal, he recognized the position that his mother had assumed in the scene of coitus he had observed. In his mind she became his mother, he was overcome by sexual excitement as that image was activated, and behaved in a manly fashion towards her like his father, whose actions he could then only have understood as urination. His urinating on the floor was actually an attempt at seduction, to which the girl responded with a threat of castration as if she had understood what he was doing.

The compulsion derived from the primal scene was transferred to this scene with Gruscha and its continued effect was mediated through it. The sexual condition underwent a modification, however, which testifies to the influence of the second scene; it was transferred from the woman's position to what she was doing in that position. This became evident, for example, in his experience with Matrona. He was walking through the village attached to their (later) estate when he saw a peasant girl kneeling at the edge of the pond, washing dirty linen in the water. He fell violently and irresistibly in love with the girl on the instant, although he could not even see her face. By virtue of her posture and her activity she had taken Gruscha's place. We can now understand how feelings of shame applying to the scene with Gruscha could be linked to the name Matrona.

We can see the compulsive influence of the scene with Gruscha at work in another attack of infatuation some years earlier. For a long time he had been attracted to a young peasant girl who was in service in the household, but had not allowed himself to approach her. One day he was seized with infatuation when he came across her alone in the room. He found her crouched down, cleaning the floor with pail and broom beside her, exactly like the other girl in his childhood.

Even his definitive choice of object, so significant in

his life, turned out to be dependent in its circumstantial details, which are not our concern here, on that same sexual condition, an offshoot of the compulsion that governed his sexual choice from the primal scene onwards, via the scene with Gruscha. I remarked earlier that I am well aware of the way in which my patient attempted to demean the object of his love. We can trace this back to a reaction against the pressure of his sister's superiority. I promised at the time, however, to demonstrate that this arrogant motive was not the only one determining his behaviour, but concealed purely erotic motives, which constituted a more profound determining force. His memory of the nursery-maid cleaning the floor, her position admittedly a demeaning one, brought this motivation to light. All the later objects of his love were substitutes for this one woman, whom a chance situation had made the first substitute for his mother. In retrospect we can easily recognize our patient's first response to the problem of his fear of the butterfly as a distant allusion to the primal scene (the fifth hour). The relationship between the scene with Gruscha and the threat of castration was confirmed by a particularly suggestive dream, which he was able to translate on his own. He said: 'I dreamed that *a man was tearing the wings off an asp [Espe]*'. 'Asp?' I naturally asked, 'What do you mean by that?' – 'Well, the insect with yellow stripes on its body, the one that can sting you. It must be a reference to Gruscha, the yellow-striped pear.' – Now I was able to correct him: 'You mean a *wasp*, then [*Wespe*].' – 'Is the word wasp? I really thought it was asp.' (Like so many others, he used his unfamiliarity with German to conceal his symptomatic actions.) 'But an asp, that must be me, S. P.' (his initials). An asp is of course a mutilated wasp. The dream tells us clearly that he is taking his revenge on Gruscha for having threatened to castrate him.

The action of the 2½-year-old boy in the scene with Gruscha is the first known effect of the primal scene, one in which he appears as a copy of his father, revealing a tendency to develop in the direction that will later merit the name 'masculine'. The seduction forces him into passivity, although we were admittedly already prepared for this by his behaviour as an onlooker during his parents' intercourse.

One aspect of the treatment history, which I must emphasize, is that in dealing with the Gruscha scene, the first experience that he could truly remember and indeed did remember without any contribution or conjecture on my part, one had the strong impression that the problem of the therapy had been solved. After this there was no more resistance; all that was needed was to gather material and piece it together. Suddenly the old trauma theory, which was after all constructed on the basis of impressions formed in the course of psychoanalytic therapy, came into its own again. Out of critical interest I made one further attempt to impose a different interpretation of his story upon my patient, one more welcome to sober common sense. I suggested that there was no reason to doubt that the scene with Gruscha had taken place, but that it meant nothing in itself; regression had caused it to seem more substantial in retrospect because of the events surrounding his choice of object, which had been diverted from his sister because of his inclination to demean and had fallen on servant-girls instead. The observation of coitus, on the other hand, might simply be a fantasy of later life, the historical kernel of which might perhaps have been the observation or experience of a harmless enema. Many readers will perhaps be of the opinion that only in making assumptions such as these had I reached a true understanding of the case; the patient looked at me uncomprehendingly and with a certain contempt as I presented this view, and never once reacted to it. I have expounded my own arguments against rationalizations of this kind above in the appropriate context.

[Not only does the Gruscha scene contain the conditions of object-choice that were to be crucial for the patient's life, however, thus guarding us against the error of over-estimating the significance of his inclination to demean women. It also enables me to justify my former refusal to trace the primal scene back to animal behaviour observed shortly before the dream, and to regard this without hesitation as the only possible solution. It surfaced spontaneously in the patient's memory without my having said or done anything. The fear of the yellow-striped butterfly, which could be traced back to it, proved that its content had been significant, or that it had subsequently become possible to invest its content with significance. We could quite confidently supply those significant elements that were no longer present to memory, by means of the accompanying associations and the conclusions suggested by them. It then transpired that his fear of the butterfly was entirely analogous to his fear of the wolf, and in both cases was a fear of castration, initially directed towards the person who had first voiced the castration threat but then transferred on to the person to whom it must adhere according to the phylogenetic model. The scene with Gruscha occurred when he was 2½; the anxiety he experienced at the sight of the yellow butterfly must have been after the anxiety-dream, however. It would be readily comprehensible if his later sense of the possibility of castration had latched on to the scene with Gruscha and generated anxiety from it; but the scene itself contains nothing offensive or improbable, only details of an entirely banal nature that there was no reason to doubt. There is nothing to encourage us to trace them back to the child's fantasy; indeed, it would hardly seem possible to do so.

The question now arises as to whether we are justified in seeing proof of his sexual excitement in the fact that the boy urinated in a standing position while the girl was kneeling on the floor, cleaning it. If so, his excitement would testify to the influence of an earlier impression, which could just as easily be the actual occurrence of the primal scene as something he watched animals do before the age of 2½. Or was the situation entirely harmless, the child emptying his bladder purely a matter of accident, and the whole scene imbued with sexuality only later on, in his memory, once he had recognized the significance of similar situations?

I do not think I am able to come to any conclusion here. I must say that I think it greatly to the credit of psychoanalysis that it can even ask questions such as these. But I cannot deny that the scene with Gruscha, the role it played in analysis and the effects it had on my patient's life can be explained most naturally and fully if we affirm the reality of the primal scene, which at other times might be seen as the product of fantasy. There is nothing fundamentally impossible in what it asserts, and the assumption that it was a reality is entirely in keeping with the stimulating influence of his observations of animals, to which the sheepdogs in the dream-image allude.

I shall turn from this unsatisfying conclusion to a question I explore in my *Introductory Lectures on Psychoanalysis*. I should very much like to know myself whether my patient's primal scene was a fantasy or a real experience, but taking other, similar cases into consideration we are obliged to conclude that it is not actually very important to reach a verdict on this matter. Scenes where parental intercourse is observed, scenes of childhood seduction and the threat of castration are undoubtedly inherited property, a phylogenetic inheritance, but they could just as well have been acquired by personal experience. The seduction of my patient by his older sister was an indisputable reality; why not the observation of his parents' coitus, too?

In the primal history of neurosis we see that the child resorts to this phylogenetic experience when his own experience is not enough. He fills out the gaps in individual truth with pre-historic truth, putting ancestral experience in the place of his own. In acknowledging this phylogenetic inheritance I am in complete agreement with Jung (*Die Psychologie der unbewußten Prozesse* [*The Psychology of Unconscious Processes*], 1917, a work published too late to influence my own *Lectures*), but I consider it methodologically incorrect to resort to a phylogenetic explanation before one has exhausted the possibilities of ontogenesis; I do not see why we should obstinately deny the pre-history of childhood a significance that we readily concede to ancestral pre-history; I cannot overlook the fact that phylogenetic motives and products are themselves in need of the light that can be shed on them in a whole series of instances drawn from individual childhoods; and finally, it does not surprise me to find that when the same conditions remain in force they again cause the same things to come about organically in the individual as they had done in ancient times, and which they then passed down in the form of a disposition to reacquire them over and over again.

The interval between the primal scene and the seduction (18 months – 3¼ years) is also where we must place the mute water-carrier, who was a father-substitute for my patient just as Gruscha was a mother-substitute. I do not think we are justified in referring here to an inclination to demean, even though both parents are represented by members of the servant class. The child takes no notice of social distinctions, which mean very little to him as yet, putting even quite lowly people on a level with his parents if they respond to him lovingly in the same way that his parents do. Equally, this inclination is of little significance when it comes to using animals as substitutes for his parents, for nothing could be further from the child's mind than to hold animals in low esteem. There is no thought of demeaning them when uncles and aunts are enlisted as parent-substitutes, a procedure attested by many of our patient's memories.

In the same period there are vague tidings of a phase

during which he only wanted to eat sweets, so that concern was expressed for his physical well-being. He was told of an uncle who had not wanted to eat anything either and who wasted away at an early age. He also heard that he had been so seriously ill when he was three months old that they had made his shroud in readiness. They succeeded in making him so fearful that he started to eat again; later in his childhood he even took this obligation to extremes, as if to shield himself against the threat of death. His fear of dying, summoned up for his own protection, came into evidence again later, when his mother issued a warning about the danger of dysentery; later still it provoked an attack of obsessive-compulsive neurosis. At a later stage we shall attempt to look into its origins and significance.

I would wish to claim that the eating disorder is significant as the very first instance of neurotic illness in my patient; thus the eating disorder, the wolf phobia and the compulsive piety represent the full range of infantile illnesses that predispose the individual to neurotic breakdown in the years after puberty. It will be objected that few children altogether avoid disorders such as a passing unwillingness to eat or an animal phobia. This is an argument I welcome, however. I am prepared to assert that every adult neurosis builds on childhood neurosis, but that the latter is not always powerful enough to attract attention and to be recognized as such. The objection only enhances the theoretical significance of the infantile neuroses for our understanding of those illnesses that we treat as neuroses and believe to be derived only from what affects us in later life. If our patient had not picked up compulsive piety in addition to his eating disorder and his animal phobia, his story would not be noticeably different from that of any other living soul and we would have missed out on valuable material that could keep us from making obvious mistakes.

The analysis would be unsatisfactory if it did not enable us to understand the lament in which our patient summed up his sense of suffering. He said that for him the world was shrouded in a veil, and psychoanalytic training leads us to dismiss any expectation that these words might be meaningless or accidental. The veil was only torn apart – oddly enough – in one situation, namely when, after the application of an enema, stools were passed through the anus. He would then feel well again and for a very short while would see the world clearly. Understanding the meaning of this 'veil' was as difficult as understanding his fear of the butterfly. He did not insist on its being a veil, moreover, and it became even more elusive to him, a feeling of twilight, 'ténèbres', and other such intangibles.

It was only shortly before leaving therapy that he recalled having heard that he had been born with a caul. For this reason he had always considered himself to be particularly lucky, a child whom no ill could befall. This confidence only left him when he was obliged to acknowledge that his gonorrhoeal illness had done serious damage to his body. He broke down in the face of this insult to his narcissism. We might say that this was the repetition of a mechanism that had come into play once before. The wolf phobia, too, had broken out when he was forced to confront the fact that castration was indeed possible, and for him gonorrhoea was clearly on a par with castration.

The veil shrouding him from the world and shrouding the world from him was thus the caul. His lament is in fact the fulfilment of a wish-fantasy in which he is shown as having returned to the womb: a wish-fantasy, admittedly, of flight from the world. We might translate it thus: my life is so unhappy that I must go back to my mother's womb.

What is the meaning of the fact that this symbolic veil, once a real veil, is torn apart, however, at the very moment when the bowels are evacuated after a clyster [enema] and that his illness abates under these conditions? The context permits us to reply: when the birth veil is torn apart, he sees the world and is re-born. The stool is the baby, and as that baby he is born a second time to a happier life. This is the fantasy of re-birth to which Jung recently drew our attention and to which he attributed such a dominant position in the wishful fantasies of the neurotic individual.

That would be all very well, if it were a complete response. Certain details of the situation, together with the consideration that there should be a connection with the particular facts of our patient's life history, require us to take our interpretation further. The condition of re-birth is that a man administers a clyster (only later, when absolutely necessary, did he perform this function himself). This can only mean that he has identified himself with the mother, the man plays the role of his father, the clyster reproduces the act of copulation, which bears fruit in the birth of the stool-baby – that is, of himself.

The fantasy of re-birth is thus intimately bound up with the condition of sexual satisfaction received from a man. Our translation now runs as follows: only when he is allowed to take the woman's place, to substitute himself for his mother in order to gain satisfaction from his father and bear a child for him, does his illness abate. Here the fantasy of re-birth is merely the mutilated, censored reproduction of his homosexual wish-fantasy.

If we look more closely, we must in fact recognize that, by setting this condition for his cure, the patient is simply reproducing the situation found in the so-called primal scene: at the time he wanted to take on his mother's attributes and in that scene he himself produced the stool-baby, as we had long ago supposed. As if spell-bound, his inner gaze is fixed on the scene that was to be decisive for his sexual life, the recurrence of which, that night of the dream, inaugurated his illness. The veil tearing is analogous to his eyes unclosing, to the window opening. The primal scene has been remodelled as the condition imposed for his cure.

We can easily take what is represented in the patient's lament, and what is represented by the exception to the condition he laments, and draw them together to form a single entity whose full meaning is then revealed. He wishes he were back in his mother's womb not simply in order to be re-born, but so as to be reached by his father during coitus, to gain satisfaction from him, to bear him a child.

To be born of his father, as he at first supposed, to gain sexual satisfaction from him, to give him a child, even if that means surrendering his manhood, and to express all this in the language of anal eroticism: with these wishes the wheel of his fixed obsession with his father comes full circle, in them his homosexuality finds its highest and most intimate expression.

In my opinion this example sheds some light on the meaning and origin of fantasies of the womb and of re-birth. The former frequently stems from an attachment to the father, as in our case. There is a desire to be in the mother's womb so as to act as her substitute during coi-tus, to take her place with the father. As a rule the fantasy of re-birth probably constitutes a euphemism, so to speak, a toning-down of the fantasy of incestuous intercourse with the mother, an *anagogic* abbreviation of it, to bor-row H. Silberer's expression. There is a desire to return to the situation in which one was in the mother's geni-tals; here the man identifies himself with his penis and uses it to represent his whole self. Thus it is revealed that each of the two fantasies is the counterpart of the other, expressing the wish for sexual intercourse with the mother or the father, depending on whether the individual con-cerned adopts a male or female attitude. We cannot dis-count the possibility that both fantasies, and hence both incestuous wishes, are united in our patient's lament and in the condition set for his cure.

Once again I shall attempt to re-interpret the latest results of the analysis according to the model preferred by my opponents: the patient laments his flight from the world in a typical womb-fantasy, glimpses the possibility of cure only in re-birth, as typically understood. He expresses the latter through anal symptoms appropriate to his dominant predisposition. According to the model of anal fantasies of re-birth he constructs a childhood scene that recapitulates his wishes using archaic symbols as the medium of expression. His symptoms are then interlinked in such a way that they appear to proceed from a primal scene of this kind. He was forced to embark on this whole line of retreat because he came up against a task in real life that he was too lazy to solve, or because he had every reason to mistrust his inferior attributes and thought this the best way of protecting himself against being passed over.

This would be all well and good if the unhappy man had not been only 4 years old at the time of the dream with which his neurosis began, the stimulus for which was his grandfather's story about the tailor and the wolf, and the interpretation of which necessitates the assumption of a primal scene of this kind. The relief that Jung's and Adler's theories might have afforded us comes to grief in the face of these petty but inviolable facts. As things are, it seems to me more likely that the fantasy of re-birth issues from the primal scene than the other way round, that the primal scene reflects the fantasy of re-birth. Perhaps we may also assume that four years after his birth the patient was just a little too young to be wishing for re-birth already. Yet I must withdraw this last argument, for my own observations prove that we have under-estimated children and are no longer able to say just what they are capable of.

IX
Recapitulations and Problems

I do not know whether my readers will have succeeded in forming a clear picture of the genesis and development of my patient's state of illness from the report of the analysis given above. Indeed, I fear that this will not be the case. However, whereas I never normally boast of my own narrative skills, on this occasion I should like to plead mitigating circumstances. To initiate the reader into a description of such early phases and such profound strata of a patient's inner life is a problem which has never before been tackled, and it is better to solve it badly than to take to one's heels, particularly since losing heart presents certain dangers in itself. Better, then, to make a bold show of not having been put off by consciousness of one's own deficiencies.

The case itself was not a particularly auspicious one. The very thing that made it possible to gain such a wealth of information about the patient's childhood, the fact that we could study the child through the medium of the adult, was bought at the price of the most dreadful fragmentation of the analysis and a corresponding incompleteness in my account of it. Aspects of personality, a national character which is alien to our own, made it difficult to empathize with him. The contrast between the patient's charming and responsive personality, his sharp intelligence and refined way of thinking, and his complete lack of restraint at the level of the drives made it necessary to spend an excessively long time on the work of preparation and education, thus rendering any kind of overview more difficult. Though it may have posed the hardest descriptive problems, however, the patient himself cannot be held responsible for the nature of the case. In adult psychology we have happily succeeded in separating the processes of the inner life into conscious and unconscious, and describing both in clear language. As far as the child is concerned, however, this distinction almost gives way. We are often at a loss to decide what we would describe as conscious, and what unconscious. Processes that have become dominant and that, given their later behaviour, we must treat in the same way as conscious ones, were nevertheless not conscious in the child. We can easily understand why this is so: consciousness in the child has not yet developed its full range of characteristics and is not yet entirely capable of being converted into language-pictures. The way in which we are regularly guilty of confusing the phenomenon of something appearing in consciousness in the form of a perception, and something belonging to an accepted psychic system that we ought to call by some conventional name but for which we also use the term consciousness (System *Cs*), such confusion is harmless in the psychological description of an adult, but misleading in the case of a small child. To introduce the concept of the 'preconscious' does not help much here, for there is no reason why the child's pre-consciousness should be congruent with the adult's. We must therefore be content with having clearly recognized the obscurity which confronts us.

A case such as the one described here could obviously create an opportunity to embark on a discussion of all the results and problems of psychoanalysis. It would be an endless undertaking, and one quite without justification. We have to tell ourselves that we cannot discover everything, cannot decide everything on the basis of a single case and that we must be content to use it for what it can show us most clearly. The task of explanation in psychoanalysis is in any case narrowly circumscribed. What we need to explain are conspicuous symptom formations, by revealing how they have come about; what we are not to explain, only describe, are the psychic mechanisms and drive processes that we encounter in doing so. Formulation of new general statements on the basis of what we have learned about these last-named aspects requires numerous cases of this kind, analysed accurately and in depth. They are not easy to come by, for each individual case requires years of work. Thus progress in these areas will only take place very slowly. There is an obvious temptation, of course, to content oneself with 'scratching the psychic surface' of a number of individuals and replacing neglected effort with speculation advanced under the patronage of some philosophical school of thought or other. There are also practical necessities that can be urged in favour of such a procedure, but the necessities of scholarship cannot be satisfied by any surrogate.

I want to attempt to sketch out a synthesis, an overall view of my patient's sexual development, beginning with the earliest indications. The first thing we hear about him is of a loss of pleasure in eating that I would interpret on the basis of other experiences, but nevertheless with circumspection, as the outcome of an occurrence in the sexual sphere. I had thus to consider the first recognizable mode of sexual organization to be the so-called *cannibal* or *oral* mode of organization, in which the scene is dominated by the original dependence of sexual excitement on the drive to eat. We cannot expect to find any direct expression of this phase, but may find some indications in the appearance of disorders. The impairment of the drive to eat – which may of course have other causes as well – draws our attention to the fact that the organism has not succeeded in controlling sexual excitement. The sexual objective in this phase could only be cannibalism, eating; in our patient's case this comes to the fore as a result of regression from a higher level, in his fear of being gobbled up by the wolf. We had to translate this fear as that of being taken in coitus by the father. It is well known that at a much later stage, in girls going through puberty or slightly older, we encounter a neurosis that expresses the rejection of sexuality through anorexia; a connection may be drawn with the oral phase of sexuality. We encounter the erotic objective of the oral mode of organization once again at the height of paroxysms of love ('I love you so much I could eat you') and in affectionate contact with small children, in which the adult himself behaves in an infantile fashion. Elsewhere I have expressed the suspicion that our patient's father himself inclined to 'affectionate scolding', and when playing at wolves or dogs with the little boy had threatened in jest to gobble him up. The patient only provided confirmation of this view through his striking behaviour in the transference. Whenever he retreated from difficulties in the therapy and sought refuge in transference, he would threaten to gobble me up, and later to subject me to every possible form of ill-treatment, all of which was merely a way of expressing his affection.

His linguistic usage has been permanently coloured in certain ways by this oral phase of sexuality: he refers to 'luscious' love-objects, describes his beloved as 'sweet'. We recall that as a child our patient only wanted sweet things to eat. When they occur in dreams sweeties and bonbons generally stand for caresses and sexual satisfaction.

It appears that there is also an anxiety that belongs in this phase (where there is a disorder, of course), which manifests itself in the form of generalized anxiety and may adhere to anything that is suggested to the child as appropriate. In our patient's case it was used to teach him to overcome his reluctance to eat, to overcompensate for it, indeed. We are led to the possible source of his eating disorder when we recall – basing ourselves on the assumption we have discussed in such detail – that his observation of coitus, which was belatedly to cast so many ripples, took place at the age of 18 months, certainly before the period at which he experienced eating difficulties. We may perhaps assume that it speeded up the processes of sexual maturity, so that it also took effect directly, if inconspicuously.

I know, of course, that we can also explain the symptoms manifested during this period, his fear of the wolf, his eating disorder, in a different, more straightforward way that takes no account of sexuality or of a pre-genital stage of sexual organization. Anyone who likes to ignore the signs of neurosis and the logical connections between phenomena will prefer this other explanation, and I shall not be able to prevent him from doing so. It is difficult to find out anything compelling about these initial stages of sexuality other than by taking the roundabout routes I have indicated.

The scene with Gruscha (at the age of 2½) shows our young patient embarking on a development that merits recognition as a normal one, except perhaps that it is somewhat premature: identification with the father, eroticism of the bladder as a substitute for virility. It too is very strongly influenced by the primal scene. Up until now we have interpreted the identification with the father as a narcissistic one, but bearing in mind the content of the primal scene we cannot deny that it already corresponds to the stage of genital organization. The male genitals have begun to play their part and will continue to do so under the influence of his sister's seduction.

We gain the impression, however, that the seduction not only encourages this development but also, to a greater extent, disrupts and diverts it. It results in a passive sexual objective that is fundamentally irreconcilable with the action of the male genitals. The first external impediment, Nanja's suggestion of castration, leads to the breakdown (at the age of 3½) of the still precarious mode of genital organization, and regression to the previous stage of anal-sadistic organization, which he might perhaps otherwise have passed through with only the same slight symptoms as those found in other children.

It is easy to recognize that the anal-sadistic mode of organization is a continuation of the oral one. The violent muscular activity towards its object by which it is characterized falls into place as an act preparatory to eating, but eating is no longer present as a sexual objective. The preparatory act becomes an objective in its own right. What is new about it in comparison with the previous stage is the fact that the receptive, passive organ has now been separated off from the oral zone, and developed in the anal zone instead. Biological parallels suggest themselves, as does the interpretation of pre-genital human modes of organization as the residue of arrangements that have been permanently retained in many classes of animal. Equally characteristic of this stage is the way in which the exploratory drive constitutes itself from its component elements.

Anal eroticism is not conspicuously in evidence. Under the influence of sadism faeces have exchanged their affectionate meaning for an aggressive one. A feeling of guilt, which indicates, moreover, that developments are taking place in areas other than the sexual sphere, plays its part in the transformation of sadism into masochism.

The seduction continues to exert an influence, in that it maintains the passivity of the sexual objective. It now transforms sadism to a great extent into its passive counterpart, masochism. It is doubtful whether we can put the boy's characteristic passivity entirely down to the seduction, for his reaction to the observation of coitus at the age of 18 months was already predominantly a passive one. The sexual excitement that he felt in observation was expressed in a bowel movement, in which we must admittedly recognize an active element. Sadism, which finds active expression in tormenting small creatures, continues to exist alongside the masochism that dominates his sexual aspirations and is expressed in his fantasies. From the time of the seduction onwards his sexual curiosity has been stirred, and is essentially directed towards two problems, namely where babies come from and whether loss of the genitals is possible; it becomes bound up with the expression of his drives. It is this that focuses his sadistic tendencies on those tiny creatures, which he sees as representing tiny children.

Our description has taken us almost up to his fourth birthday, at which point the dream causes the observation of coitus at the age of 18 months to come belatedly into effect. We can neither completely grasp nor adequately describe the processes that are now set in motion. The activation of that image, which thanks to advances in his intellectual development can now be understood, has the effect of a newly occurring event, but is also like a fresh trauma, an alien intrusion analogous to the seduction. The genital mode of organization, which had been suspended, is resumed at a stroke, but the progress made in the dream cannot be maintained. Rather, a process that can only be compared to a kind of repression causes him to reject this new knowledge and replace it with a phobia.

Thus the anal-sadistic mode of organization continues in existence, even during the animal phobia phase that now begins, but with some manifestations of anxiety mixed in. The child still pursues both sadistic and masochistic activities, while reacting fearfully against one component; the reversal of sadism into its opposite probably fares somewhat better.

We can see from the analysis of the anxiety dream that repression follows immediately after the knowledge of castration. The new knowledge is rejected because to accept it would cost the boy his penis. More careful consideration reveals something like the following: what has been repressed is the homosexual attitude in the genital sense, which had been formed under the influence of the new knowledge. This attitude remains preserved in the unconscious, however, constituted as a deeper, closed-off stratum. The driving force behind this repression appears to be the narcissistic masculinity of the genitals that comes into conflict with the passivity of the homosexual objective, a conflict for which the ground was laid long before. Repression is thus one of the outcomes of masculinity.

This might lead us into the temptation to revise one small aspect of psychoanalytic theory. It seems patently obvious, after all, that repression and the formation of neuroses proceed from the conflict between masculine and feminine aspirations, that is, from bisexuality. But such a view has its shortcomings. Of these two conflicting sexual impulses one is acceptable to the I [*Ichgerecht*], the other offends against narcissistic interests and thus falls prey to repression. In this case, too, it is the I [*Ich*] who sets repression in motion in favour of one of the two sexual aspirations. In other cases, such a conflict between masculinity and femininity does not exist; there is a single sexual aspiration present, which sues for acceptance but runs counter to certain powers of the I and is therefore banished. Far more frequent than conflicts within sexuality itself are those conflicts that arise between sexuality and the moral inclinations of the I. There is an absence of moral conflict of this kind in our case. To emphasize bisexuality as the motivation for repression would be too restrictive, whereas conflict between the I and the sexual aspirations (the libido) covers all eventualities.

Against the theory of 'masculine protest' as developed by Adler, it must be objected that repression by no means always upholds masculinity against femininity; in many whole categories of cases it is masculinity that is obliged to accept repression by the I.

A more balanced evaluation of the process of repression in our particular case, incidentally, would challenge whether narcissistic masculinity is significant as the only motivating factor. The homosexual attitude that comes into being in the course of the dream is so powerful that the little boy's I fails to control it and fends it off through the process of repression. To achieve this end the I enlists the help of the narcissistic masculinity of the genitals that is in opposition to the homosexual attitude. Simply in order to avoid any misunderstanding let me state that all narcissistic impulses work out from the I and remain in the I's domain, while repression is directed towards those objects carrying a libidinal charge.

Let us now turn from the process of repression, a notion we have perhaps not succeeded in mastering entirely, to the boy's state when he awakened from the dream. If it had indeed been masculinity that had triumphed over homosexuality (femininity) during the dream process we should now find an active sexual aspiration, already explicitly masculine in character, to be the dominant one. There is no question of this, however: the essential nature of the mode of sexual organization is unchanged, the anal-sadistic phase still continues in existence and remains dominant. The triumph of masculinity can only be seen in the fact that the boy reacts fearfully to the passive sexual objectives of the dominant mode of organization (which are masochistic, but not feminine). There is no triumphant masculine sexual impulse present, but only a passive one, and an unwillingness to accept it.

I can imagine the difficulties that this sharp distinction between the active/masculine and passive/feminine will cause the reader, a distinction that is unfamiliar but essential to our purpose, and so I shall not hesitate to repeat myself. We can describe the state of affairs after the dream, then, as follows: the patient's sexual aspirations have been split, the genital mode of organization having been achieved in the unconscious and a highly intensive homosexuality constituted; above this (virtually at the level of consciousness) the earlier sadistic and predominantly masochistic sexual current continues to exist, while the I has altered its position, by and large, towards sexuality, anxiously rejecting the dominant masochistic objectives just as it reacted towards the deeper homosexual ones with the formation of a phobia. Thus the outcome of the dream was not so much the victory of a masculine current as reaction against a feminine, passive one. We would do violence to the facts if we ascribed masculine characteristics to this reaction. For the I does not have sexual aspirations, only an interest in self-protection and the preservation of its narcissism.

Let us now look closely at the phobia. It came into existence at the level of genital organization and demonstrates the relatively simple mechanism of an anxiety-hysteria. The I protects itself from something it judges to be excessively dangerous, that is, homosexual satisfaction, by developing anxiety. However, the process of repression leaves a trace that we cannot miss. The object to which the dreaded sexual objective has become attached must find representation in conscious thought by means of another. It is not fear of the *father* that comes to consciousness, but fear of the *wolf*. Once it has been formed, the phobia is not restricted to a single content. Some considerable time later the wolf is replaced by a lion. Sadistic impulses towards tiny creatures compete with a phobic response towards them, inasmuch as they represent the boy's rivals, the babies whose arrival is still possible. The genesis of the butterfly phobia is particularly interesting. It is like a repetition of the mechanism that generated the wolf phobia in the dream. A chance stimulus activates an old experience, the scene with Gruscha, whose castration threat belatedly comes into effect, whereas at the time it appeared to have left no impression.

We can say that the fear that goes into the formation of these phobias is fear of castration. This statement in no way contradicts the view that the fear arises from the repression of homosexual libido. Both modes of expression refer to the same process, in which the I withdraws libido from the homosexual wish-impulse, which is converted into free-floating anxiety and then allows itself to be bound up in phobias. It is merely that the first mode of expression also indicates the motive that drives the I to act in this way.

Looking more carefully, we then find that the random choice of a single phobia does not represent the full extent of this first episode of illness (not counting the eating disorder) in our patient, but that it must be understood as a genuine case of hysteria, comprising both anxiety symptoms and conversion phenomena. An element of the homosexual impulse is retained by the organ involved, for henceforward, and in later years too, the bowel behaves like an organ that has been hysterically affected. The unconscious, repressed homosexuality withdraws into the bowel. It was this particular bit of hysteria that served us so well when it came to resolving the patient's later illness.

Now we should steel ourselves to tackle the still more complicated circumstances of the obsessive-compulsive neurosis. Let us examine the situation once again: a dominant masochistic sexual current and a repressed homosexual one, opposed to an I that is caught up in hysterical refusal; what processes could transform this state into one of obsessive-compulsive neurosis?

The transformation is not the spontaneous result of internal developments, but arises from an external, alien influence. Its visible outcome is that the boy's relationship to his father, still very much to the fore, and expressed up until then through the wolf phobia, now finds expression in compulsive piety. I cannot let this opportunity pass without pointing out that the process that our patient undergoes provides unambiguous confirmation of a claim I put forward in *Totem and Taboo* concerning the relationship of the totemic animal to the deity. There I concluded that the idea of God does not develop out of the totem but arises independently from common roots to supersede it. The totem is the first father-substitute, the god a later one in which the father regains human form. We find the same thing in our patient's case. He goes through the stage of the totemic father-substitute, as represented by the wolf phobia, which is then broken off and, after a new relationship has been forged between the boy and his father, is replaced by a phase of religious piety.

The influence behind this transformation is his acquaintance with religious doctrine and sacred history, arranged by his mother. The result is exactly the one that education aspires to. The sado-masochistic mode of sexual organization draws gradually to a close, the wolf phobia quickly disappears and in the place of his frightened rejection of sexuality we find a higher form of sexual suppression. Piety becomes the dominant power in the child's life. These efforts of will are not achieved without a struggle, however: its signs are the appearance of blasphemous thoughts and its consequence the onset of a compulsive exaggeration of religious ritual.

Leaving aside these pathological phenomena, we can say that, in this case, religion has achieved everything it is employed to do in the education of the individual. It has curbed his sexual aspirations by offering sublimation and a safe anchor, and undermined his family relationships, thus preventing the isolation that threatens him by giving him access to the wider human community. The unruly, apprehensive child has become socially conscious, civilized and educable.

The principal driving force behind the religious influence was his identification with the figure of Christ, which readily suggested itself given the coincidence of his date of birth. The excessive love for his father that had made repression necessary could finally be channelled into an ideal sublimation. It was possible as Christ to love the father, now called God, with an intensity that he had striven in vain to vent on his own earthly father. The ways in which this love could be attested were clearly indicated by religion and no guilt adhered to them, whereas there was no way of separating guilt from the erotic aspirations of the individual. While the patient's deepest sexual current, already laid down as unconscious homosexuality, could still be drained off in this way, his more superficial masochistic aspirations lost very little in finding a sublimation without parallel in the Passion of Christ, who had allowed himself to be mistreated and sacrificed on behalf of the divine father and to his greater glory. And so religion did its work in this boy who had gone off the rails, through the mixture of satisfaction, sublimation, diversion from sensual processes to purely spiritual ones, and the opening up of social relationships which it offers the believer.

His initial reluctance to accept religion was derived from three different sources. First, it was simply his way to ward off anything new: we have already seen a number of examples of this. Once he had taken up a given libido position he would defend it every time against the new one he was to occupy, fearful of what he would lose in giving it up and mistrusting the likelihood of finding a fully satisfactory substitute. This is an important and fundamental psychological particularity, which I put forward in *Three Essays on the Theory of Sexuality* as the capacity to become *fixed*. Referring to it as psychic 'lassitude', Jung sees it as the principal cause of all neurotic failure. I believe he is wrong to do so, for it is more far-reaching than this and has a significant part to play even in the lives of those untouched by neurosis. The fluidity or viscosity of libidinal energy charges, and of other types as well, is a particular characteristic found in many normal individuals and not even in all those of a neurotic disposition, and up until now no connection has been made between it and anything else, as if it were a prime number which cannot be divided any further. We know only one thing: the mobility of psychic charges is a property which dwindles noticeably with age. This provides us with one of the indicators for the limits of psychoanalytic influence. There are people, however, whose psychic plasticity is maintained far beyond the usual limits of age and others who lose it very early on. If these are neurotic individuals then we discover to our discomfort that in their case, under what are apparently the same conditions, it is impossible to reverse changes that can readily be controlled in others. In examining conversion in psychic processes we must therefore give consideration to the concept of an *entropy*, which is in proportional opposition to the undoing of what has already taken place.

A second target was provided by the fact that there is no single, clear relationship to God the Father underlying religious doctrine; on the contrary it is shot through with signs of the ambivalent attitude that prevailed at its inception. His own highly developed ambivalence enabled him to sniff this out and use it as a starting-point for the penetrating criticism that so astonished us in a 4-year-old child. Most significant of all, however, was undoubtedly a third factor to which we may ascribe the pathological effects of his battle against religion. The current of energy pressing him towards manhood, for which religion was to provide a form of sublimation, was no longer free, as part of it had been separated off by the process of repression and thus eluded sublimation, remaining bound to its original sexual objective. On the strength of their connection the repressed part strove either to break through to the sublimated part or else to drag it down to its own level. Those first brooding thoughts circling around the person of Christ already contained the question as to whether this sublime son could also fulfil the sexual relationship to his father that the patient had retained in his unconscious. Repudiation of this endeavour resulted only in the emergence of apparently blasphemous compulsive thoughts in which physical tenderness for God continued to assert itself in a form intended to demean Him. A violent struggle [*Abwehrkampf*] to parry these compromise formations led inevitably to compulsive exaggeration of all those activities in which piety and the pure love of God found expression through the prescribed channels. The victory eventually fell to religion, but the way in which it was rooted in the drives proved incomparably stronger than the durability of what was produced by sublimation. As soon as life provided a new father-substitute whose influence was directed against religion, it was dropped and replaced by other things. We should also bear in mind the interesting complication that piety came about under the influence of women (mother and nurse) whereas masculine influence liberated him from it.

The fact that obsessive-compulsive neurosis came about at the anal-sadistic stage of sexual organization on the whole confirms the views presented elsewhere in 'Die Disposition zur Zwangsneurose' ['The Disposition to Obsessional Neurosis'] (1913). However, the pre-existence of a powerful state of hysteria makes the case more obscure in that respect. I shall conclude my survey of our patient's sexual development by highlighting the transformations it underwent in later life. In puberty the strongly sensual male current that we refer to as normal made its appearance, its sexual objective that of the genital mode of organization, and its vicissitudes fill up the time until his later episode of illness. It was directly connected with the Gruscha scene and derived from it the character of a compulsive infatuation, coming and going like an attack; it also had to struggle with the inhibitions created by the residue of the infantile neurosis. Violent breakthrough to the female meant that he finally won his full masculinity; from now on he held fast to this sexual object, but its possession brought him little joy, for a strong and now completely unconscious inclination towards the male, the sum of all the energies generated in earlier phases, was constantly drawing him away from a female object, obliging him to exaggerate his dependence on women in the interstices. His complaint in therapy was that he could not endure being with women, and all our work was directed towards the task of uncovering his unconscious relationship to the male. We could say, in a formulaic way, that the hallmark of his childhood was vacillation between the active and the passive, that of puberty the struggle for manhood and that of the period following his illness, the fight for the object of male aspirations. The cause of his illness does not come into any of the categories of 'neurotic illness' that I might refer to collectively as special cases of 'refusal' [*Versagung*] and so draws our attention to a gap in this series. He broke down when an organic infection of the genitals re-awakened his fear of castration, damaged his narcissism and forced him to put away any expectation that Fate had a personal preference for him. The cause of his illness was thus a narcissistic 'refusal'. His excessively strong narcissism was in complete accord with the other indications of inhibited sexual development: with the fact that his choice of heterosexuality, however energetic, was the focus for so few of his psychic aspirations, and also that the homosexual attitude, which is so much closer to narcissism, asserted its unconscious power over him with such tenacity. In the face of such disorders, psychoanalytic therapy obviously cannot bring about an instantaneous change of direction nor parity with normal development; it can only remove obstacles and clear the paths so that life's influences can opt for better directions in which to push through the individual's development.

Let me list those peculiarities of his psyche that were uncovered in psychoanalytic therapy but on which it was not possible to throw further light nor exert any direct influence: the tenacity with which his energies became fixed, as already discussed, the extraordinary extent to which his tendency to ambivalence had been developed, and, a third feature of what we might term an archaic constitution, his ability to maintain a wide variety of violently conflicting libidinal charges, all potentially functioning alongside one another. His constant wavering between them, which for a long time seemed to exclude the possibility of settlement and progress, dominated the profile of his later illness, which we have touched on only briefly here. There is no doubt that this was a character trait of the unconscious, carried over into processes that had become conscious; it was only apparent, however, in the results of emotional [*affektiv*] impulses, whereas in matters of pure logic he demonstrated particular skill in detecting contradictions and inconsistencies. The impression left by his inner life was rather like that of the ancient Egyptian religion, which is inconceivable to us because it conserves all the developmental stages alongside the end-products, keeping the oldest deities and what they signified as well as the most recent, spreading them out two-dimensionally where other developing cultures create a three-dimensional image.

This concludes what I wished to say about this case. Only two of the numerous problems to which it gives rise seem to me to deserve particular emphasis. The first concerns those phylogenetically transmitted patterns that, like philosophical 'categories', enable us to accommodate our impressions of life. I should like to suggest that they are the precipitates of human cultural history. The Oedipus complex, a complete account of the child's relationship to his parents, is one example, indeed the best-known. When experiences cannot be fitted into this hereditary schema, they are reworked in the imagination, work that it would undoubtedly be profitable to examine in detail. For it is precisely these cases that are best suited to demonstrate the independent existence of the schema. We are often in a position to note how the schema takes precedence over individual experience, as for example in our case when the father becomes the castrator who threatens childhood sexuality, despite the fact that the Oedipus complex is reversed in every other respect. Another effect of this is seen when the children's nurse takes the place of the mother or the two become merged. The way in which experience contradicts the schema supplies the conflicts of infancy with a wealth of material.

The second problem is not far removed from the first, but its significance is far greater. If we consider the way in which the 4-year-old child responds to the reactivated primal scene – indeed, we have only to think of the far simpler reactions of the 18-month-old child to the original experience – it is difficult to dismiss the notion that some kind of knowledge that resists definition, a sort of preparation for understanding, is at work in the child. What this might consist in defies the imagination; the only analogy available to us is the excellent analogy with the largely *instinctive* knowledge found in animals.

If human beings were also in possession of instinctive knowledge of this kind, it would hardly be surprising if it were directed in particular towards the processes of sexuality, although it cannot possibly be restricted to these alone. This instinctive knowledge would form the core of the unconscious, a primitive intellectual activity later dethroned by human reason when this is acquired and overlaid by it, but often, perhaps always, retaining the strength to drag higher inner processes down to its own level. Repression would be the return to this instinctive stage; in this way man would pay for his splendid new acquisition with the capacity for neurosis, while the possibility of neurosis would testify to the existence of the earlier, preliminary stage, instinctive in nature. The significance of early childhood traumas would then lie in the fact that they supply this unconscious part of the psyche with material that prevents it from being sapped by the subsequent process of development.

I know that similar thoughts have been expressed in various quarters, emphasizing the hereditary, phylo-genetically acquired factor in the individual's inner life; indeed, I think we are all too ready to make room for them in our psychoanalytic evaluations. It seems to me that they are only admissible when psychoanalysis correctly observes the prescribed stages, and only starts looking for traces of what has been inherited once it has penetrated the layers of what has been acquired by the individual.

(1918 [1914])

THE STORY OF PENGUIN CLASSICS

Before 1946 ... 'Classics' are mainly the domain of academics and students; readable editions for everyone else are almost unheard of. This all changes when a little-known classicist, E. V. Rieu, presents Penguin founder Allen Lane with the translation of Homer's *Odyssey* that he has been working on in his spare time.

1946 Penguin Classics debuts with *The Odyssey*, which promptly sells three million copies. Suddenly, classics are no longer for the privileged few.

1950s Rieu, now series editor, turns to professional writers for the best modern, readable translations, including Dorothy L. Sayers's *Inferno* and Robert Graves's unexpurgated *Twelve Caesars*.

1960s The Classics are given the distinctive black covers that have remained a constant throughout the life of the series. Rieu retires in 1964, hailing the Penguin Classics list as 'the greatest educative force of the twentieth century.'

1970s A new generation of translators swells the Penguin Classics ranks, introducing readers of English to classics of world literature from more than twenty languages. The list grows to encompass more history, philosophy, science, religion and politics.

1980s The Penguin American Library launches with titles such as *Uncle Tom's Cabin*, and joins forces with Penguin Classics to provide the most comprehensive library of world literature available from any paperback publisher.

1990s The launch of Penguin Audiobooks brings the classics to a listening audience for the first time, and in 1999 the worldwide launch of the Penguin Classics website extends their reach to the global online community.

The 21st Century Penguin Classics are completely redesigned for the first time in nearly twenty years. This world-famous series now consists of more than 1300 titles, making the widest range of the best books ever written available to millions – and constantly redefining what makes a 'classic'.

The Odyssey continues ...

The best books ever written

PENGUIN (🐧) CLASSICS

SINCE 1946

Find out more at www.penguinclassics.com